Cabs, Companies & Characters

Story of the Edinburgh Taxi Trade

Bob McCulloch

Published by New Generation Publishing in 2021

Copyright © Bob McCulloch 2021

First Edition

The author asserts the moral right under the Copyright, Designs and Patents Act 1988 to be identified as the author of this work.

All Rights reserved. No part of this publication may be reproduced, stored in a retrieval system or transmitted, in any form or by any means without the prior consent of the author, nor be otherwise circulated in any form of binding or cover other than that which it is published and without a similar condition being imposed on the subsequent purchaser.

ISBN   978-1-80031-055-1

www.newgeneration-publishing.com

New Generation Publishing

Cover photo

from right to left
1992 Fairway 1937 Austin Jones Fishtail 1957 Beardmore 2018 LEVC TXE

In memory of Jim Haynes whose help and advice was inspirational

With thanks to

Bill Munro, a retired London cabbie and publisher of books on the iconic London taxi, for permission to quote from his book Carbodies: The Complete Story

Rab Fairgrieve for his knowledge of Central Radio Taxis

Rab Veitch for sharing his memories

Ann Meikle and Norma Walker for their help with the manuscript.

Joyce for her unending support

Thank you to Saskia Osterloff and all production staff at New Generation Publishing for their help and advice.

All proceeds go to Onecitytrust

Foreword

The History of the Taxi Trade in Edinburgh

Bob McCulloch's, "The History of the Taxi Trade in Edinburgh" is absorbing, fascinating, and an insightful and enjoyable read.

The author's skilfulness in describing the way technological advancements, and societal changes have impacted upon the trade throughout its long history, informs and stimulates the reader; and further enhances the affection and esteem within which Edinburgh's Taxi Trade is widely and rightly held.

The history of the Taxi Trade in Scotland's capital city reaches back to when sedan chairs were available in Edinburgh for public hire, to the origins of the renowned annual Edinburgh Taxi Children's Outing.

All aspects of the Taxi Trade in Edinburgh and how they have evolved and come to be are warmly described - from the Hansom Cab; to how taximeters were invented and introduced; to why Brougham Street and Brougham Place are so named.

Learning about various "well kent" characters who have led, shaped and determined the direction and make-up of Edinburgh's Taxi Trade over the years; and reading the stories captured in "Tales From The Rank" entertains and amuses.

A strong sense of the camaraderie and sporting competitiveness within the trade is epitomised in the exploits of past Football Teams and Golf Outings.

Throughout its existence, people working in Edinburgh's Taxi Trade: operators; drivers; people taking bookings and despatching jobs have been valued ambassadors for our city.

Providing a safe, reliable, wholly accessible, low emission, door to door public transport service of the highest standard is what the Edinburgh Taxi Trade provides residents and visitors alike.

The establishing of customised Taxi Tour Guiding courses a few years ago by the author for Edinburgh's taxi drivers has proved to be a pioneering and popular initiative. It also brought about the matriculation of the Coat of Arms of The Worshipful Company of Hackney Carriage Drivers by the Court of The Lord Lyon.

As with countless business sectors, the Edinburgh Taxi Trade has been hard hit by the impact of the Coronavirus pandemic.

Looking to the future, as we move slowly and cautiously towards economic recovery, and as leisure and business tourists return to "Auld Reekie", the option to explore and experience Edinburgh via a Taxi Tour Guide is a safe, appealing, attractive and sustainable one, respectful of current social distancing guidelines.

I heartily commend this important and fascinating History of Edinburgh's Taxi Trade by Bob McCulloch, and wish every reader, an enjoyable 'journey through the pages'.

Lezley Marion Cameron

Contents

Chapter 1: Introduction 1
Chapter 2: Chairmen 5
Chapter 3: Taxi Meters 9
Chapter 4: Conditions of Fitness 12
Chapter 5: Cab Stances.. 17
Chapter 6: Carbodies 23
Chapter 7: Companies 30
Chapter 8: Controllers 52
Chapter 9: Main Dealers... 56
Chapter 10: Vehicles... 58
Chapter 11: Cab Inspectors 83
Chapter 12: Cab Trade Legends 92
Chapter 13: Independent Taxi Services 108
Chapter 14: Taxi Regulations 112
Chapter 15: Ecatra Football..................................... 115
Chapter 16: Ecatra Golf.. 124
Chapter 17: Childrens Outing................................. 128
Chapter 18: Worshipful Company Hackney Carriage Drivers 141
Chapter 19: A Magical Trip with a Special Boy..... 143
Chapter 20: Tales from the Rank............................ 146
Chapter 21: Conclusion.. 192

History of Edinburgh Taxi Trade

Chapter 1

Introduction

Having been involved in the cab trade in Edinburgh for over 40 years, 35 years as an owner in City Cabs, I have seen many changes, not always for the better, to the way the trade operates.

Drivers nowadays are more insular and less willing to socialise with their compatriots preferring to use social media to communicate with each other, leading to a situation where they do not know each others names. But it was not always like this, drivers mixed socially and if anyone needed help, someone was always there. The fun seems to have gone from the trade and the characters have all departed, never to return. It is a sad reflection on the trade when many "old timers" say they are glad to be out of it and nothing would entice them back behind the wheel at a time when the trade needs all the help it can get.

In the 1950's, taxi owners opened up a club on Granville Terrace and named it after their vehicle, the Austin Club. You had to be a taxi owner to gain membership, but due to dwindling membership the club closed and the building was converted into flats.

The Taxi Club, which started in Broughton Street Lane, before taking over the Bookmakers club on Beaverhall Road, is still managing to keep going but like many other social clubs, its future looks uncertain.

The licensed Hackney Carriage trade in Britain has a long history. It was first established in London. In 1636, King Charles I made a proclamation to enable 50 hackney carriages to ply for hire in London. After the Civil War in

1654, Oliver Cromwell set up the 'Fellowship of Master Hackney Carriages' by Act of Parliament, and hackney driving became a profession.

This makes the licensed taxi trade the oldest regulated public transport system in the world and it is the people in the trade who have demanded that it be this way. The rivalry between licensed and unlicensed hire vehicles has been around for as long as the taxi trade.

The trade in London is regulated by the Metropolitan Police, who operate the Public Carriage Office (PCO) and who determine the conditions of fitness (C.O.F.) of both vehicles and drivers. This soon spread to provincial cities where they chose which of the conditions would apply to them. Edinburgh has followed closely to the edicts of the PCO. The cab office, now called the Taxi Examination Centre, is where all vehicles must go for their annual inspection. This is part MOT and part compliance, and any vehicle failing to meet the very high standards demanded, are issued with "a red sticker" stating that the vehicle must not be used for public hire until the faults have been rectified. As well as annual inspections, the inspectors carry out random road side checks. Smaller towns have chosen to reject the purpose built vehicle and in some cases even the topographical test. To obtain your green badge in London is an achievement comparable to a university degree. Edinburgh has long been second only to London in the high standards required to be a taxi driver.

Alongside the topographical test, the potential taxi driver must sit modules covering everything from licensing conditions, health and safety, first aid and customer awareness.

The cost of these modules is borne by the applicant. As well as a medical, applicants must undergo a thorough police check, with radio companies insisting that their members have a Disclosure Scotland certificate for dealing with vulnerable people. The cost of obtaining the certificate is borne by the applicant.

The trade has evolved from sedan chairs to horse drawn vehicles, and later to motorised vehicles with a variety of makes culminating in the electric vehicle of today. The trade has seen many changes but none so potentially damaging as the uncontrolled explosion of private hire numbers.

The 2020 Covid-19 pandemic saw the trade virtually shut down with many owners and drivers leaving the trade completely.

The taxi trade is unique in that it has always done amazing charity work.

No other trade or organization has done the same for the same length of time. Many members of the trade spend a lot of unpaid hours organizing help for the disadvantaged in our society. Nearly all major cities and some smaller towns hold children's outings, trips to the seaside or Christmas parties. Surely the jewel in the crown must be the Magical Taxi Tour, run by The Worshipful Company of Hackney Carriage Drivers, where one hundred London taxis take over two hundred children with life limiting illnesses on a weekend to Euro Disney. In 2005 my son Neil and I were the first drivers from Scotland to make the trip. This is something I would repeat a further thirteen times and my son doing many more. As my son did not own a cab, he asked Billy Paton for the loan of a demonstrator for a charity trip. Billy readily agreed and as the cab was in Aberdeen, ordered it to be brought to Edinburgh straight away. My son then said to Billy, "You never asked where we are going, but it is to Paris." His response was, "I hope you have a great time. We will make sure the tank is full." Billy then gave us cash to buy sweets for the children.

As the cost for each cab making the trip was £1,000, Neil and I went round the ranks and garages asking for sponsorship. In a week we raised £2,500 which we presented to the organizers. Due to the generosity of the Edinburgh cabbies, this started a very close relationship between the drivers of both capitals. Many London taxis take veterans to visit World War two sites, or Poppycabs take veterans to Remembrance Services. As well as trips, cabbies supply warm clothing, sleeping bags and toiletries to the homeless. The money to provide these services is raised by volunteers, some climbed Mt. Everest, others chose to cycle across the Sahara, while others held fund raising nights out.

No driver is looking for thanks for these acts of charity. It is done for the good name of the trade and the people involved should be justly proud of themselves.

None walks so tall as those who stoop to help the less fortunate in our society.

Chapter 2

Chairmen

Public hire vehicles date back to the Roman Empire when chariots were used to transport people for a fee.

Filthy streets littered with mud, refuse and excrement were not only a health hazard in 16th and 17th century Europe, but also made travel difficult and impractical, until the introduction of the sedan chair, that is.

A 17th Century traveller, Saunders Dunscombe, saw sedan chairs (which were named after the town Sedan, in France where they were first used) being used in Italy and realized a commercial opportunity and imported a number for use in London. It was not long after that, entrepreneurs were petitioning King James II and VII to grant them a franchise for Scotland.

Sedan Chair

Sedan chairs for public hire were first introduced to Edinburgh on 19th. October 1687, when six were licensed. Prior to these, horse drawn coaches were used but these proved impractical due to the narrow closes and steep gradients of the Old Town, so the sedan chair was a particularly suitable form of transport. The hackney chairs were made of wood and covered in black leather with a cushioned seat and a door at the front. Adaptations were made to suit the particular environs of Edinburgh, these included a door at the side to allow easy access in the narrow confines of the closes and wynds. Another adaptation was a seat on a pivot that allowed the passenger to remain horizontal whilst travelling up or down steep inclines. Privately owned chairs were much more elaborately decorated with embossed leather work, painted pastoral scenes inside, embroidered seats and intricate metal work.

The eighteenth Century saw the peak of sedan chair use, from the original six in 1687. By 1780 the number had risen to 180 hackney chairs and 50 privately owned. By 1814 the number had dropped to 101 and the decline continued.

1827 saw the number further reduced to 46 and by 1850 horse drawn carriages had replaced almost all chairs. The last chair stance was at the corner of Great King Street and Dundas Street which operated until around 1870.

At the peak of sedan chair popularity there were 152 Chairmasters (people who owned the chairs) and 156 Chairbearers (people who carried them) with 8 odd men (people who carried a chair on a part time basis). Also licensed were 16 military Chairmasters owning 33 chairs employing 24 Chairmen. The military chairs would only operate from military premises such as the Castle.

The Chairmen of Edinburgh were at one time a numerous and well employed body of men and some were known to amass large sums of money. Donald McGlashan, a Chairmaster who resided in Mylnes Square off the Lawnmarket, employed 12 men. It is said that he amassed a small fortune lending money to young men of rank whose remittance had run low. He never charged interest but was always rewarded in kind.

Before a chairman received authorization from the council to work within the City, a prominent Burgess had to act as security for them by signing a "Bond of Caution" which was effectively a guarantee of behaviour, which was witnessed by a Bailie.

The practice continues today. Before a new member to the trade can drive a taxi, his application must be signed by two Councillors.

The sedan chairs were a fairly dignified form of transport as long as the user was in no great hurry and the distance to be travelled was not great, but they were extremely uncomfortable when the Chairmen were busy as they would set off at a fast trot and as the carrying poles were quite pliant, the extreme bobbing up and down and the swinging from side to side caused a type of motion sickness.

Chairmen

Chairman Donald Black standing Chairman Donald Kennedy seated
etching by John Kay

The majority of Chairbearers were Highlanders who were displaced due to the Highland Clearances and their uniforms were mostly clan tartan. They were issued with a badge showing two Chairmen carrying a chair with their motto

"Honesty is the Best Policy" round the border and topped with a crown.

It was a quaint form of transport used mainly by ladies to visit dancing assemblies or the theatre. For an extra charge they could have a lantern inside and a pan of hot water under the seat. Another extra was a link boy, who would walk in front carrying a flaming torch to light the way.

The main stance was at the Tron Kirk. A table of fares introduced in 1738, stipulated sixpence (2 ½ p.) a trip in the City, four shillings (20p) for a full day's hire and one shilling and sixpence (7 ½ p) for the distance of a mile and a half outside the city boundary. Their tariff for 1810 was, hired from 10am. - midnight, seven shillings and sixpence (38p) 9am. -4pm. three shillings and sixpence (18p.).

The eccentric High Court Judge, Lord Monboddo, would hire a chair when it rained, not for himself, but to transport his wig whilst he walked alongside.

The opening up of the New Town saw the demise of the sedan chair as the New Town was better suited to coaches.

The last sedan chair garage is still to be seen in Tweeddale Close off the High Street opposite John Knox's house. A sedan chair is on show at the Royal Museum of Scotland on Chambers Street.

Sedan Chair Garage

Chapter 3

Taxi Meters

In the days of horse drawn coaches, the fare was calculated from a cab stance to a set destination, ie. Ettrick Road to Haymarket Station for one or two passengers 1/- (5p), three or four passengers 1/6 (7 ½ p). Each driver was supplied with a list of prices in his Hackney Carriage Bye laws.

The first recorded device for measuring the distance a vehicle travelled was used in ancient Rome where a mechanism used the turning of the wheels to release small wooden balls. At the end of a journey the amount the passenger paid was based on how many balls had been released.

The term taxicab was not used before the introduction of taximeters in 1907, the term being derived from the words taximeter cabrioles, soon shortened to taxi cabs. The word taximeter is an adaptation of the German taxameter, which is coined from the Medieval Latin, taxa which means charge and the Greek word metron meaning measure. In 1891 a German nobleman, Baron von Thurn und Taxis set up a company delivering mail. So that his customers would know how much to pay, he designed a device that recorded the number of revolutions the wheel of the coach made. The modern taximeter that calculates the fare on a combination of time and distance was invented by Wilhelm Bruhn and the first meter equipped cab was the Daimler Victoria, built by Gottleib Daimler in 1897 and operated in Stuttgart. The first taximeters were introduced to London in 1907 and were fitted to both horse drawn and motor cabs. The mechanical meter worked on a combination of time and distance; to calculate the fare it had a clock that had to be wound up by hand to measure the time and a cable from the gear box to measure distance. If the cabbie forgot to wind up the clock, the fare would only be calculated on distance.

When the meter was in the hired position, a ticking sound came from the meter and when it stopped the cabbie would try to wind it up with the passenger on board. Part of the meter was a lever with a square plate attached called the flag. When the vehicle was for hire, the lever was in the upright position, and when hired, the driver swung the lever downwards to set the meter running and from this we get the term "the drop of the flag." At the end of the journey the cabman moved the lever again and a bell sounded to let the passenger know that the meter was in the stopped position. The early meters were supplied on a rental basis from the British Taximeter Company at a rental fee of £8 per annum, Halda a Swedish company for £6 10/- per annum or Halls garage in Roseburn, who were the agents for the Bell Punch Meter Company at £6 per annum.

Bell Punch Meter   Halda Meter

When a tariff change occurred, the cabbie had to go to the agents to have his meter re-calibrated and then go to the cab office to have it checked and sealed to prevent tampering. A common problem arose when the cabbie would be informed that his meter was 'one or two yards out and creeping,' meaning that the initial distance was wrong and each subsequent yardage was getting shorter. He then had to go back to the agents to have the fault rectified before going back to the cab office. It was not unknown for a cabbie to go through this procedure several times. With 480 meters to be re-calibrated, it would take a week before the tariff change was completed. In the 1980's, the introduction of electronic meters put an end to this. Many companies brought out electronic meters which the cabbie could buy, among them Lucas, Argo, Sheriff, Novax, Halda and Cavalier.

When replacing his cab the owner had to transfer his meter to his new cab, this practice died out in 1994 when John Paton & Son started supplying Cygnus meters in new cabs and became the main agent in Scotland for Cygnus.

City Cabs who had obtained the agency for Sheriff meters in 1981, saw the demand for new meters begin to drop and passed on the agency to Chris Skinner (V180) who had been garage manager at East London Street. Chris set up Edinburgh Taxi Meters (ETM) in August 1998. Many changes have taken place in the electronic meter industry with mergers, takeovers and company restructuring. Sheriff became Wayfarer, which became Lucas-Tronic. In 2006 Lucas-Tronic appointed ETM as main distributor to supply and assist other dealers in southern Scotland, as well as north to Dundee and as far west as the West Coast. Also that year ETM took over as main agent for Digitax in the Edinburgh area.

Chapter 4

Conditions of Fitness

Contrary to what has become an urban myth, it has never been a requirement for a cabbie to carry a bale of hay, although he was required to carry sufficient oats to feed the horse during his shift.

With the introduction of motor vehicles into the cab trade, the Public Carriage Office (P.C.O.) a division of the Metropolitan Police Force laid down a set of specially written rules for vehicles which would be licensed to ply for hire on the streets of the Capital.

Edinburgh, along with other major cities adopted some of the Metropolitan Conditions of Fitness (C.O.F.) to govern the licensed taxi trade. Most were sensible and designed to protect the travelling public, but others do not stand up to close scrutiny and were subject to individual interpretation by Licensing Officers.

Probably the most well known one is the 25ft. turning circle. This was introduced so that cabs could reverse direction without using forward and reverse gears where the engine may be stalled causing the driver to leave the vehicle and hand crank the engine causing delays to other road users.

The rules also required enough headroom in the cab that allowed a gentleman to wear a top hat whilst seated and if travelling in a four - seat cab, allow sufficient knee room so that if a gentleman was seated opposite a lady, their knees would not touch.

Another rule demanded the separation of driver and passengers. This was included because in the words of Chief Superintendent Bassom, head of the P.C.O. who laid down the rules, "Cabs are not like private motors where the owner knows the class of person he has beside the driver, but public carriages are frequently used by persons who are more hilarious than wise...getting beside the driver and interfering with the mechanism...so as to be a source of danger to themselves and others using the road".

No hub caps were allowed. The reason given was that wheel nuts could be checked at a glance, also, no cover over the fuel cap for the same reason, and in this instance, the rule still applies.

One of the more ludicrous was the 10 inch ground clearance rule. This was to prevent anyone who had been knocked down, suffering further damage as the cab ran over him. The development of the motor car meant that the C.O.F. were reviewed in 1927 when the ground clearance was dropped to seven inches and in 1938, a window was allowed in the driver's door.

In 1960 the FX3 four door cab was rejected by the cab inspector, despite having gained approval in London. It would later gain approval.

Edinburgh abandoned the turning circle requirement in June 2006 allowing the introduction of what became known as alternative vehicles or van conversions

Hackney Coaches

Hansom Cab

The Hansom Cab was invented and patented by Joseph Hansom in 1834. It was because of their manoeuvrability that they quickly replaced the Hackney Carriage. At the height of their popularity there were 7,500 in use in London and their popularity quickly spread to other cities.

It was originally known as the Hansom Safety Cab and in its name lies the reason for its success. Other cabs of the time had stability problems which made them prone to overturning. Hansom overcame this and resolved the safety issue without compromising on speed.

In fact, it was because of this speed that it was the carriage of choice for the fictional detective Sherlock Homes. Its speed and manoeuvrability made it the ideal vehicle for Arthur Conan Doyle's famous detective, allowing him to arrive at crime scenes quickly.

The Hansom cab prospered until cheap motorized transport and the construction of transport systems saw more people using cars and the cab fell into decline.

By 1927, there were just 12 Hansoms licensed in London and the last London Hansom cab driver turned in his license in 1947.

Brougham Carriage

Henry Brougham born in St. Andrew Square in 1788, invented the Brougham Carriage which was built by coach builder Robinson & Cook. They became very popular with the gentry and when upgraded by their owners, were then used as a public hire vehicle. Brougham Street and Brougham Place are named after him.

Hackney Coaches were first known in Edinburgh 1673 and the first regulations were introduced in 1685.

By 1840 there were 82 Hackney Coaches licensed.

The cost of a badge to coachmen and chairmen in 1849 was to be set at a sum sufficient to reimburse the council for the expense of printing their regulations.

Before a person could be licensed to drive a Hackney, he had to get a cautioner, which is someone who would sign an affidavit guaranteeing the applicants good behaviour. The applicant could only drive so long as his cautioner remained alive, was resident in the city or did not withdraw. Records show that Mr. Alexander Millar, a draper of 20 Bristo Street, withdrew as a cautioner for a William Riggs on January 15th 1866. Riggs had his license revoked that day.

Bye laws for 1880 state that "Every driver shall, during the hours of divine service on Sundays or other days set apart for public worship by lawful authority, drive at walking pace whilst passing any place of public worship."

Drivers of horse drawn coaches had to be a hardy bunch. They were out in all weathers and with no protection from the elements. It is therefore not surprising that so many were charged with being drunk in charge of a horse, some as many as thirty times.

On the 30th. March 1884, George McCulloch, 166 Canongate, was charged with being drunk and incapable, he was admonished.

Thomas Beggen of 45 Cumberland Street, in November 1887, was found to be "Drunk and incapable" at the Stockbridge stance. Sheriff Rutherford found him guilty and he was fined 5/- (25p) or one day in the gaol. As it was his first conviction, he had his license restored by Bailie Roberts on the sight of the Total Abstinence Pledge.

In February 1885, George Sawers, of 9 Raeburn Place, was charged with congregating (over ranking). Bailie Turnbull fined him 5/- (25p) or three days in the house of correction. As he did not have the money, he took the three days in gaol. It was his 12th conviction.

Robert Young was charged on the 31st. March 1885, with "furious driving".

He was fined 7/6 (37 ½ p) or three days in gaol. As it was his first offence, Bailie Roberts quashed the sentence on hearing that he had enlisted in the Scots Greys.

Female taxi drivers are a relatively new addition to the trade. Up to the late 1970's, there was only one, Tina Tait, who was an owner in Central Radio Taxis.

1979 saw the first female apply to join City Cabs as a driver, only to be met with the comment "Over my dead body!" from the then chairman, Dougie Logan.

It was only after the threat of legal proceedings and advice from other committee members that she was allowed in the company as a driver.

There was an attempt to prevent women working night shift and the advice from cab inspector Rutherford was unambiguous "Why not? Women police officers patrol the streets at night."

Over the next period of time more and more women joined the trade, often passing the topographical test as a result of helping their husband's to study. Others realizing the economic benefits, became partners in what had been a traditional male occupation.

Chapter 5

Cab Stances

A 19th Century report from the Scotsman newspaper stated
Shelter For Cabmen

A most important movement has commenced in Edinburgh to afford shelter for cabmen.

Through the exertions of Mr. A. B. Fleming, designed by Mr. Pilkington, and provided by subscriptions by inhabitants of the neighbourhood, and the cabmen themselves, a new wooden building has been erected at the stand in Randolph Crescent. Large side views command a full view of the road in each direction and entry is by a door from the street side immediately facing the stand. A gas stove will be provided to heat the building and there will be a boiler for the supply of hot water. If shelter such as this in Edinburgh had been provided for cabmen in every town there would be less encouragement to intemperance, and the cabmen's calling would be rendered in every respect more healthy. If, as a medical contemporary suggests, these stands were each provided with a restaurant where good food was provided, the movement would prove a still greater boon to the poor cabby.

In the late 19th. century, Hackney Carriages were licensed to work from assigned stances with set numbers for each stance. Coachmen had to apply to the magistrates for permission to move to another stance when a vacancy arose.

On 28th. May 1917, there having been no cabs working from the Stockbridge stance for a considerable time, the cabmen's shelter was removed by order of Bailie Boyd. This following a letter submitted by a Mr. Charles A. Stevenson, 28 Douglas Crescent, requesting its removal.

A petition from cab owners was made on 4th June 1923, for the retention of a two cab stance at the north end of

Lothian Road. The Magistrates agreed but stipulated one must be motor and the other horse drawn for a trial period of three months. This arrangement was made permanent on 24th September 1923.

Most cab stances had a cab shelter where coachmen could shelter from the elements whilst waiting on a fare. These were equipped with a table, chairs and a gas ring for boiling a kettle.

A bequest by Mr. William Crambe Reid of 28 Blacket Place, of £1000 for the repair and upkeep of cabmen's shelters was made on 1st.December 1922. The Magistrates agreed to administer the bequest.

Canonmills Stance.

On the 16th. January1910, records show that cab operator Mr. Player, having withdrawn his cabs from this stance and the stance now being unoccupied, the shelter was removed to Tynecastle yards, McLeod Street, for storage. In the Council minutes for 16th. May 1916, there is a request to move the cab shelter from St. Vincent Street to Atholl Crescent. As there were only 4 men working the stance, they found the shelter too large and expensive to maintain so asked for it to be substituted with a smaller one.

Belford Bridge Stance removed 1912.

On 28th. December 1915 the cabmen's shelter was moved from Castle Terrace to Chamberlian Road.

Cabman's shelter south side of Lauriston Place

This shelter, which is said to be the oldest in the City, being at least forty years old, has been allowed to fall into a state of disrepair and decay, due to the cabbies not having occupied it for at least eighteen months. On the 7th. August 1915, the shelter was struck by a passing vehicle, demolishing the North West corner, making the shelter beyond repair. As there were only 6 cabs working the stance and the drivers said they never used the shelter as it is no use to them in its present condition, and they have no money in fund to repair it, supposing it was possible to do so, they wished it removed. After a visit from Bailie McArthy and the Assistant Hackney Carriage Inspector they were satisfied that it was beyond repair and granted permission for its removal.

On the 2nd. March 1923, the Burgh Engineer was instructed to remove the shelter from Gayfield Square and replace it with one from North West Circus Place. Bailie Hutchison, on the 30th. January 1921, authorized the removal of the shelter from the Goldenacre stance on Inverleith Row as only 1 cab was working the stance.

Grange Stance at the East end of Grange Road.

Alex Duncan's cabs, which were the only ones which stood on this stance were sold off on 22nd May 1912, and the stance being left unoccupied, the cabman's shelter was removed by the Burgh Engineer. The shelter was in such a dilapidated state that it was broken up.

Cabman's shelter Morrison Street

In Council minutes dated 8th. August 1919, it is recorded that having been unoccupied for several years, that the shelter having fallen into a dilapidated and objectionable condition, and boys or other persons unknown, having broken all twelve windows and completely wrecked the interior, it was decided that the shelter should be broken up by the Burgh Engineer. On the 13th. December 1929, representation was made to the Magistrates by cabmen who stood on the Morrison Street stance asking if they might be granted the use of the Weigh House at Haymarket as a shelter or that a shelter be placed on the stance. The

Magistrates were not prepared to break into "Capital of Bequest" to provide a shelter.

On 30th November 1930, the Hackney Carriage Inspector met with the Inspector of Lighting and Cleansing and requested that Hackney Carriage drivers working Morrison Street stance would have the privilege of using as a shelter the old Weigh House which was presently being used by the Cleansing Department for storage and by the scavengers of the district. This privilege was granted.

Kilgraston Road Stance.

John Croall & Son, Coachbuilder, who had premises on Castle Terrace, introduced the first motor cab in the city around 1907. Their fleet would eventually rise to 17 motor vehicles. They withdrew their cabs in April 1916 from this rank owing to the First World War. Croall informed the Magistrates that he intended to occupy the rank after the war with both horse drawn and motor cabs. However, in 1920 Croall informed the Magistrates that he would not again work cabs from this rank. Subsequently, Bailie Robertson authorized the removal of the shelter which was carried out on 22nd. July 1922.

London Road Stance.

John Logue, driving for Dan T. Munro informed Council that as he was the only cab working from this rank and never after 8pm, he could not guarantee the safety of the shelter. As the condition of the shelter was in a dilapidated and ruinous condition and being used as a convenience by people of the night, the Magistrates ordered its removal. It was removed on 5th. November 1917.

On 16th. October 1918, Chamberlain Road shelter was removed to London Road. The shelter was repaired out of the Reid bequest in April 1923.

In April 1923, Lynedoch Place shelter was in such a ruinous condition it was removed and replaced with the one from Clarendon Crescent. Hackney Carriage drivers who paid 2/6 (12 ½p) per annum were T. Anderson, J. Dickson (plate no 676), W. Forrest (1176), B. Inlay (817), J. Goodsir (1060), G. Hoy (738), A. McInnes (532), A. Nisbet (1151), J. Plews(965), J. Ovenstone (921) and N. Wishart (1117)

On 27th.December 1915, the shelter at Barclay Place was in such a state of disrepair that it was demolished and replaced with the one from Chamberlain Road.

The shelter on Whitehouse Loan was removed and given to the Parks Department on 22nd. July 1920. It remains in use at Barclay Terrace as the starters box on Bruntsfield Links short hole golf course.

Cabmans Shelter

In 1926, the cab stances on Princes Street were reversed from East to West facing.

The 1910 regulations required a turning circle of 25ft. The tariff for horse drawn coaches was 8d (3p.) for the first mile and 4d. (1 ½ p) for every half mile thereafter, for motor coach's 1/- (5p) for the first mile and 2d (1p) for each subsequent quarter mile with double fare between midnight and 7am.

At the southern end of the Dean Bridge stands Kirkbrae House, which housed Stewarts Cab Office. James Stewart lived there from 1860 until his death, aged 87 in 1917. A jovial, bearded gentleman, who always wore a top hat, ran his cab business from here. In keeping with his advancing years, instead of going to the cab rank at the junction of Queensferry Street and Randolph Crescent, a distance of one hundred yards to inform the cabbies of their pick-ups, he would simply shout out the orders to the cabmen. On the front door step of the house is a brass plate which reads Stewarts Cab Office.

As the trade moved from horse drawn to motorised vehicles these shelters were no longer a necessary requirement.

Kirkbrae House

Chapter 6

Carbodies

It's ironical to think that one of the world's most recognizable cars and indeed a British icon - the FX4 taxi, was built in a virtually unknown car maker's factory.

It was one that went on to change the face of the cab trade in Britain.

Love them or hate them, they produced a taxi that is recognized and loved the world over both by sight and sound.

Nearly everyone in the country could recognize the sound of the engine, the sound of the doors closing and the familiar squeal of the brakes. Which was handy, when on a radio job the customer would come out and tell the driver "I heard you coming."

Robert "Bobby" Jones was apprenticed to Lawson's of Manchester as a coach body builder. Lawson enjoyed the reputation of being one of the finest coach builders in England. When he finished his apprenticeship in 1894, Bobby continued in the coach building trade. As more and more motor cars began to appear on the streets Bobby realized that this was where the future lay.

In 1904, he secured a job with Humber at their factory in Beeston in Nottingham, gaining invaluable experience in running a factory. In 1919, Bobby joined Gooderman & Co., a timber merchant in Coventry. Gooderman & Co. wished to move into the motorcar body building business and Bobby ran the production line. Within two years, the opportunity to buy the business arose and Bobby jumped at it. He approached Bill Dawson, one of the earliest employees at Gooderman's, to become his partner, but Dawson could not raise the money so he took on a Mr. Tooby Adkins - Soobroy as a sleeping partner for a few years. Bill Dawson was a pattern maker, who with his son cycled from their home in Aberdeen to Coventry seeking work. Despite being unable to become a partner he would go on to be an integral part of the company, as did his son and grandson.

Moving into new premises in 1921, he named the company Robert Jones trading as Carbodies. This was done to avoid confusion as there was already a coach builder called Jones.

Bobby Jones who stood only five feet tall and endowed with great mental fortitude soon earned a reputation as a hard task master. He is remembered by former employees as something of a tartar who would not tolerate unions, smoking, late arrival or drinking tea outside official teabreaks. Employees have told that when passing through the factory, if he spotted a tea-can boiling on the stove, used to heat the premises, he would stand beside the fire until the water boiled away and the tea-can was burned. A sheet metal worker on his first day at work, placed his tin tea mug and his hammer on his work bench as Bobby walked past. Picking up the hammer he smashed the mug with the words "You are here to work so you will not be needing that." Yet he is also remembered as a true friend who was good to his workers. Indeed, it is said that if you survived the first month you had a job for life. There was no set day wage in the factory; Jones followed the coach building tradition of fixing a price for a job.

The benefits were equally advantageous to him and the workforce. He knew how much each body would cost and for the work force, the more bodies they made, the more money they earned. If a rate was agreed between Bobby and the rate fixer and was subsequently found to be too low or too high, there was no way Bobby could be persuaded to change it. An example of this was a welder whose job was to tack weld door skins for taxis. Securing them to the door frames, he was paid 2/- (10p) a door. As he could do twenty an hour, that made his wage £80 for a forty hour week and that was in 1954. At the end of his shift he would exchange overalls for a suit and drive home in a Jaguar.

Bobby Jones would never turn any work away and found a niche as a sub-contractor that the big companies could not fill. This was making bodies for a vast range of car manufactures such as Alvis, Daimler, Morris, Rootes Group and Rover, whose production levels were not very high.

With the name Bobby Jones, it is no wonder that Bobby was a golf addict, even going so far in 1933 as to name the Rover four door sports car the "Fairway," a name that would be resurrected in Carbodies future.

During the war the factory was turned over to armaments work and was making body frames for lorries and ambulances as well as the gun turrets for bomber aircraft.

In 1943, Carbodies became a limited company with Bobby retaining a 90% stake and his son Ernest, the remaining 10%. This was probably done to secure industrial equipment under the lease lend agreement as up until then the company had been Robert Jones trading as Carbodies and part of the lease lend agreement was that equipment went to *bona fide* companies and not individuals.

In 1945 a massive blow was dealt to the company. The Inland Revenue, claiming that they had made excessive profits during the war gave them a crippling tax bill. Out of a net profit of £122,000, they were left with just over £1,200.

They applied for a refund and the Ministry for Aircraft Production stated that Carbodies was one of the few firms that did not grossly over charge the government for work and services during the war. Eventually the Exchequer relented and £100,000 was returned to Carbodies. With a new tool room and money to invest, the future was looking good, but Bobby, now in his 72nd year, was a coach builder at heart and could not grasp the changes in car production, mainly all steel bodies. Ernest, his son did understand the changes, but as he was a good office administrator and salesman, he left the day to day running of the factory in the very capable hands of Jack Orr. This did not please Bobby as he felt that Ernest should take more control of the business and have less reliance on Jack Orr. This led to many heated rows between father and son. By 1954 the situation between father and son had become untenable and Bobby decided to sell out to Birmingham Small Arms (B.S.A.) for £1000,000. Former employees have stated that Ernest knew nothing about Bobby's intention to sell up until the special board meeting on the 24th. June, when he received a cheque and Carbodies became part of the enormous B.S.A. group, alongside such illustrious names as Daimler and Lanchester. When B.S.A. representatives handed over the cheque for one million pounds, Bobby stunned all present by offering to buy the company back for one million one hundred thousand pounds, but Ernest sat silent, never backed his father up and watched as his inheritance changed hands as the deal went through. The reasons for Bobby's actions have never been made clear but it is thought he wanted Ernest to run the company by himself without the influence of outsiders. A sad end to an era.

Bobby lived for another four years and died 21st. December 1958. Ernest went on to run Bridge Clock Motors successfully until his death from inoperable cancer in March 1962.

Gun making in Warwickshire goes back to 1692 during the reign of William of Orange. King William decided that Britain should have her own arms manufacturing instead of relying on imports and he ordered 200 muskets from five Birmingham gunsmiths.

The trade flourished and in 1861 16 gunsmiths banded together to form Birmingham Small Arms Trade (B.S.A.). In times of peace when the demand for weapons fell, the company diversified into making bicycles and in 1910 produced its first motor bike. The company went from strength to strength and helped by two world wars, became one of the biggest manufacturing conglomerates in the world. However, bad management along with a failure to invest in new technology and new models, saw the company brought to its knees. In an attempt to save the British motorcycle industry, the Department of Trade and Industry stepped in and gave approval for a takeover by Manganese Bronze Holdings in 1973.Immediately after the takeover, Carbodies General Manager Bill Lucas, advised Dennis Poore, chairman of Manganese Bronze Holdings never to tell any taxi driver that he owned the company that made his vehicle as he would never hear the end of it. Poore was immensely proud of the fact he owned the company that made "Black Cabs" and disregarded Lucas's advice for the first week, but the next time he saw Lucas he said "You were right!I got into a cab and told the driver that I'd just bought the company that made his cab, and you would not believe the abuse I got."

Austin, having merged with Morris to form British Motor Corporation (B.M.C.) now became part of the British Leyland Group who had industrial relation troubles through the 1960's and 70's. It was sometimes difficult to know who was running the company, management or the trade unions. Shop steward Derek Robinson, known in the press as 'Red Robbo' could bring the workers out on strike for little or no reason, often in different parts of the production line on the same day, bringing production to a halt. It was his agenda to bring the British car industry to an end. Management were not being allowed to manage as they were constantly having to deal with stoppages. The workforce were demoralized and the product was shoddy and unreliable. British Leyland or B.L. as it became known was haemorrhaging cash. Michael Edwardes was brought in to save the company and as part of a series of cost cutting measures, the Morris Commercial plant that made the FX4 chassis had to close. At the 1970 Commercial Motor Show on the Carbodies stand, in the privacy of the back of the show vehicle, George Turnbull, Austin-Morris General Manager offered Bill Lucas the taxi chassis manufacturing plant on the understanding that Austin would remain responsible for any design changes. B.S.A.'s board approved the purchase and in 1971 the plant was transferred to Carbodies along with six men and a foreman.

Lucas had stipulated that there should be no redundancies as he did not want to upset the trade union movement, in fact the men were well pleased as they would earn more money under the Carbodies system. So, after 50 years, Carbodies were a complete vehicle manufacturer. From the launch of the Fx4 in 1958, the number of chassis built at Longbridge was 1,696 before production was moved to Adderley Park where 16,079 were manufactured. Carbodies would go on to produce 25,450, making a total of 43,225. By 1982, British Leyland were fast losing interest in taxi manufacture and handed over the intellectual rights to the FX4 to Carbodies.Another part of Edwardes cost cutting plan was to sell the engine to India as new legislation was on the way and B.L. would not spend the money on the cab to meet the new rules. The loss of the engine would have a disastrous effect on Carbodies. In May 1982, the name was changed from Austin FX4 to Carbodies FX4.Another piece of the jigsaw had fallen into place. In 1984 the owners of Mann and Overton, Lloyds Bowmaker, decided to split up the company and offered the retail side for sale and Carbodies management persuaded Dennis Poore, chairman of Manganese Bronze, to buy the company. So in 1985, London Taxis International (LTI) came into being with three divisions in the group, LTI Carbodies the manufacturer, LTI Mann & Overton the dealers, and LTI Finance, and for the first time in its history, Carbodies would have sole say on the future of taxi development.

In October 2010, the London Taxis International was rebranded as The London Taxi Company. A joint venture with Chinese car maker Geely. Also, in 2010 the Mann & Overton trading name was dropped.

In October 2012, following a suspension of sales due to the discovery of a serious flaw with vehicle steering components and having failed in an attempt to obtain new financing, the company was placed in voluntary administration.

The faulty steering components had been sourced from Geely supplier, Gang Yang in China.

In February 2013, certain assets of The London Taxi Company were purchased from administrator by Geely

It continued to trade as The London Taxi Company until rebranded as the London EV Company in September 2017, developing electric commercial vehicles at a new plant near Coventry. The first into production being an electric taxicab, the LEVC TX with the Union Motor Company being the agents.

The original Carbodies factory was demolished in 2020

London Electric Vehicle Company TXE

Chapter 7

Companies

It is a true saying that the cab trade was divided the day the second license was granted. History shows that too many owners were looking out for their own interests, which is perfectly understandable, but to the detriment of the trade in general and the refusal to accept change. It cannot be co-incidental that most of the changes in the trade have been imposed against the will of the majority of the trade. Added to this is a distrust of other taxi radio companies which are seen as rivals, when in fact they are the same people driving the same vehicles, doing the same job. It must be said that most of the animosities are historical and are no more than perceived grievances lost in the mists of time and have no place in the modern cab trade.

Much of the terminology used in the trade comes from the horse racing fraternity, plate holders are owners, drivers are jockeys, paying the rental is the weigh in and when a driver changes cabs it is referred to as changing stables, customers are referred to as punters, and working is sitting in the saddle.

In the early part of the 20th. Century the Edinburgh cab trade was dominated by large fleet owners, many having been horse coach operators. These were John Croall & Son, coachbuilder from Castle Terrace, John Player of 65 Pitt Street, John Player & Son of 25 Duke Street, George Hall of Hope Street, who had operated a Victoria Phaeton Hansom cab in 1899, Dan T. Munro, who was established in 1898, James Stewart of 10 Randolph Cliff, Robert Dickson "Braefoot," the foot of Clermiston Road, William Dunbar of Morrison Street, J.A. Cochrane of West Mayfield, John Fortune of Lochrin Place, Adam Cramond,

Peter Victory of Montgomery Street, who operated ten cabs and whose son Johnny would go on to be one of Scotland's best loved comedians, John Henderson, who operated Key Ring Cabs in Leith, and Ronald Young of Black and Yellow taxis, who operated from the Anvil garage on Peffermill Road. He stopped being an operator, becoming the main agent for taxis and had premises on Bonnington Road. He closed down in 1984.

Over the years, successive committees of the big two companies have operated a policy of mistrust of each other. This is at odds with the majority of owners/drivers who get on well together, and in an attempt to combat PHC would like to see a merger between the two companies, but despite several attempts, this has not happened.

City Cabs

On the 13th. September 1925, 25 cab owners held a meeting in the Free Gardeners Hall, on Picardy Place, to discuss the formulation of a company with the aims of

1) to abolish parking on taxi ranks

2) to supply assistance in getting road worthy vehicles through their annual inspection.

The company was named the "Edinburgh Licensed Hackney Carriage Association" and was constituted on 18th. October 1925 with an entrance fee of £1. 15/-. On the 2nd. November 1925, the fare tariff was set at 1/- (5p) for the first mile and 6d (2 ½p) every ¼ mile thereafter. One of the first things which was addressed was the need for the installation of a telephone at the rank on Princes Street; they applied to the Council but received a negative reply.

The cabbies were soon protesting against the removal of the rank at the foot of Lothian Road which was used to service the hotel and the Caledonian Railway Station. The rank was to be moved to the west side of Lothian Road, south of Castle Terrace, to allow an island to be placed in the middle of the road for tram passengers. The cabbies staged a 'sit-in' on the rank and refused to move, resulting in 15 being summoned to appear before the Magistrates on 3rd. March, 1926. All 15 were admonished.

At the annual General Meeting held on 7th. November 1926, it was proposed that premises be found with the intention of starting a phone service. The proposal was carried and premises were found on 22nd March 1927, at 44 Hanover Street, at a rent of £9 annum.

At the same meeting it was proposed that the company badge should be a white star.

In 1931 subscriptions were 2/6d (12 ½p) a week.

During the war the cab trade in Britain suffered badly. Not only were there were no new cabs available, but spares were in short supply as manufacturers had turned to war production. This led to fleet owners cannibalizing vehicles to keep others on the road. Fuel shortages were the most serious problem and in 1943 the fuel allowance was 240 gallons a month for a double shifted cab. This figure was based on 20 mpg. Cabbies complained that owing to the hilly terrain in the city, their allowance should be increased, and the President of the company met with officials of the Ministry of Fuel but to no avail.

Another problem was the blackout, where vehicles were not allowed to show lights, including panel lights during the hours of darkness. One London cabbie, when asked how he coped with blackout driving replied, "If I hit a cyclist with my nearside wing, I am too far left. If I hit one with my offside wing, I am too far right and if I don't hit anybody, I'm all right." Another cabbie, who reaching down to flick his panel lights on to check his speed ran over a policeman who stepped in front of the cab to charge the driver with speeding.

In 1946 the company made a proposal to the Council for permission to have a phone installed at the Princes Street rank. It was to be a memorial to the taxi drivers who had fallen during the Second World War. Permission was refused.

It was not until 30th. June 1948, that permission was granted for the installation of a phone at the Waterloo Place rank, 23 years after it had first been applied for.

It proved an instant success with over 300 calls in the first three days alone.

In 1949, a phone at the Tollcross rank was approved, followed by phones at the 'Foot of the Walk' rank and the Morrison Street stance; phones were also installed in the three stations. John Player and John Croall, who had the right to exclusively work the Waverley and Caledonian stations, with Halls working Haymarket, lost the franchise in May 1950 when the company became the sole contractor for the three stations for a fee of £1600 per annum. Player gave permission to the Association to use the phones in the stations and decided to end his involvement in the cab trade.

In 1951 it was decided that the phones in both the Waverley and Haymarket Stations be staffed during station hours with the calls being diverted to Waterloo Place and Morrison Street ranks during the time the office was closed. It was not unknown for cabbies to ignore the ringing of the phone, preferring to pick-up off the street, (what's new?) or cabbies not in the Association answering the phone and keeping the job for themselves. December 1951 saw the company adopt a new name, the "Edinburgh Taxicab Owners Association."

The early 1950's saw the introduction of new technology to the cab trade, radios. This idea went down like a lead balloon as the cab trade are generally a conservative group who will resist change even if it will benefit them in the long run. With the majority of the Association members, who could not see the point of paying for a radio when they could work the stations and pick up from the rank, the idea was thrown out.

On 28th. October 1952, it was decided at an A.G.M. that members with a radio should be asked to leave the Association. Each year at the A.G.M. the question of radios would be raised and each year the proposal would be defeated. At the 1955 meeting the vote was, for radios - 56, against radios - 63.

The controversy over radios in cabs would drag on for a further three years before being passed on the 16th. February 1958.

To prevent drivers out with the Association from answering the phones at stances, it was decided at the 1954 A.G.M. that drivers should be given keys to the phone boxes on a deposit of 2/6 (12 ½ p). Station dues for 1954 were £11 per annum

Other rules passed in 1954 were,

1. That no person having driven private hire would be allowed to drive in the Association.

2. No part time drivers or owners taxi driving must be full time employment.

3. No rental be given to drivers.

This rule would be passed again in 1966, the "weigh in" was strictly on a share of 'the clock,' ie, meter readings, which had to be taken at the start and end of the shift. The split was 1/3 or 6/8d (33p) in the pound, one share for the owner, one for the cab and one for the driver. This eventually changed to 60/40, with country work split 50/50. Rentals would not become the norm until de-limitation in 1984 when new owners realizing the financial implications of operating a cab were desperate to get a driver, and they were in short supply as they had taken their own issue of a plate and they were looking for a driver themselves. It got to the stage where the price of a rental did not reflect the running costs of the cab.

Some drivers secured a very good financial deal as the owner was desperate not to lose them, forgetting that drivers always need owners, owners do not always need drivers.

Ronnie Brown, who was a member of the committee was appointed representative of Westminster Insurance in 1955. At first it was limited to members of the Association but Westminster, realizing this was a limited market, insisted that it be opened to the whole trade. It was decided that he should become the agent and he opened premises at 2 Dean Path. On his death in 1973, the agency passed to his wife, who, it has to be said, did the cab trade no favours at all. Indeed, she was responsible for many owners going to other insurance companies. On her retirement in 1987, City Cabs took over the agency making her an ex gratia payment of £1000. Due to inter-company rivalry, there was no way that owners from Central Radio Taxis would put commission money into City Cabs and so Central Radio Taxis was given an agency.

Tradex Insurance Company opened an office in Edinburgh in 1995 and through a combination of competitive prices and helping the children's outing, gained a good name in the trade, leading to many owners leaving other companies to join them.

Westminster Insurance was taken over by Tradex in 2008, re-branding the name Westminster Policies with City Cabs and Central Radio Taxis retaining their agencies.

Jimmy Hopper (V17) proposed a change of name and on Tuesday the 17th. June 1958, the association changed its name to City Cabs Ltd. by a vote of 64 for - 4 against. The reason for the change was simple. Now that radios were in taxis and more people were phoning to hire them, the new name would come first in the phone book. One other proposal which seemed innocuous caused a great deal of upset. Jimmy Hopper also proposed that company cabs should have a badge on the hire sign to distinguish them from other cabs. The president told him to go ahead and design one. This he did. His design was a pennant with the name City Cabs and an image of a border keep. He asked the president to forward his design to the cab office for approval and was told "We do not need to. We tell them what is happening, they do not tell us how to run our business. Just go ahead and order them." He did this, placing an order for 100 at 10/- (50p) each, with Emslie engraving on Haddington Place. When they were fitted to the cabs, the company received a letter from the Lord Lyon informing them that the pennant was a heraldic symbol and they would have to gain his permission to use it or face a fine, so the pennants were removed. At the next general meeting, the president was censured for wasting association funds and was asked to resign. As the pennants had been a success, it was decided to design a new badge. This one would have a steering wheel against a yellow background.

As many of the association members were single shifted, they hired the radio on a single shift system, 6am - 6pm or 6pm - 6am, returning it to the office at the end of their shift.

A day shift man could hand in his radio at 6pm and work the streets or stations if he desired. As some drivers were ignoring radio work at the busy times, it was decided to introduce radio call sign numbers on windscreens to make it easier to identify which cabs were dodging radio work.

The single shift radio system was stopped in 1980.

The committee realizing that it would be a benefit to members of the association if they had their own garage premises, and so in 1959, rented the garage on Belford Road at Sunbury from Sloans for £10 a month (£120) per annum on a 10 year lease. When the filling station was up and running, they entered into an agreement with the Firestone Rubber Company to purchase taxicord tyres at £7 each with a retail price of £7 18/6 (£7.92p). It was common practice to buy tyres on hire purchase. The terms were 30/- (£1.50) down and £1 a month for six months. The total price, £7.10s with all profits going to the Association.

It was also decided that all members purchase 5 gallons of fuel per week or pay the association 3d a gallon for loss of profits. The opening hours of the filling station were 10am - 7pm and the attendant was Andrew Byers, brother in law of Ronnie Brown.

The Bell Punch meter company suggested that as their agent, Halls of Roseburn, were not open at weekends it would be beneficial to everyone if City Cabs were to appoint a mechanic to do repairs and Alfie Strathdee was duly appointed with Bell Punch paying 7/6 (37 ½ p) per fitting. The company also entered into an agreement with Carey Springs of Annandale Street to supply road springs for 32/6d (£1.62 ½ p) in an exchange scheme.

In 1960, Robert Wax of the Northern Trading Company of Manchester, entered into an agreement with the company to pay them £10 plus 5% of hire purchase commission on all new cabs sold, but in 1963 the contract was cancelled when Northern Trading were found to be a mite tardy in paying what they were due.

A big step for the company was to do away with the call boxes on the stances and stations and centralize all phone calls to one office. The membership voted to purchase 199 Morrison Street, for the sum of £1000, with the telephone numbers FOU 6336 and FOU 6131. In 1961 the company made an unsuccessful attempt to lease the former police garage on Henderson Row, but the bid failed as the City Council had it earmarked for another use. It would become the cab office in 1979 before being sold to Scottish Life, now Royal London.

When the District Council decided in 1969 to increase the number of licenses, a motion was put forward at the A.G.M. that any member accepting a new license would be asked to resign from the Association. The resulting vote was in favour of the motion.

The 1970's saw the company consolidate its position as Edinburgh's premier taxi company with many of the old guard retiring and new ideas being discussed.

In 1971, Ronnie Young of Black and Yellow taxis, decided to cease operations and apply for membership. He had his application rejected as the company was moving away from multi owners to owner drivers. He would go on to open a taxi dealership on Bonnington Road.

1974 saw the introduction of twin channel radio work, 'channel one, outer zones,' 'channel two, inner zones' with jobs being offered on a three call system, 'first call, in the street,' 'second call, in the vicinity,' 'third call acceptance call.' This was a very time-consuming business with competing cabs being measured on a map, (with, according to rank talk, a piece of elastic.)

A proposal in 1971 to start up a trade body named Edinburgh Federation of Taxi Owners with a remit to engage in dialogue with the District Council and promote the image of the trade was short-sightedly defeated.

1973 saw the introduction of a direct phone line between City Cabs and Central Radio Taxis. This was used when one company had difficulty covering a job, it could be 'blown away' to the other company if one of their cab's was in the vicinity. The advantage of this was threefold, it helped the company cover work, the customer got their cab on time, and it cut down on a driver's dead mileage saving him fuel. The direct line worked well but despite the benefits to all concerned, it was decided at committee level to withdraw this arrangement. Another example of the short sighted, parochial and insular outlook of successive committees.

With the lease on the filling station at Sunbury coming to an end, the committee began looking at other sites. Only one was found to fit all requirements and that was situated on East London Street. A rental agreement was entered into and after 4 years, the committee decided that it would be more beneficial financially to purchase the premises and this was done in 1974 with the loan being repaid in 1978. With a lubricating bay, a ramp, ample parking and wash areas, offices, a parts department and a rest room known to the trade as 'the Howf', where deals were done, rumours started, gossip exchanged, characters assassinated (in the friendliest possible manner) and where a broken down cab could be repaired for the universal charge, the price of a cup of coffee from the vending machine, (20p). It became the hub of the company where a member could find out what was happening in the trade. At the 1984 A.G.M. the membership voted for improvements to the garage, but the committee chose to make alterations that were to benefit them and to the detriment of the members, who were incensed at the plans. An Extra-ordinary General meeting was called in October and held in the Assembly Rooms, George Street, to discuss the alterations taking place at the garage. The service bay was being done away with to provide office accommodation for the chairman and the secretary. After a heated discussion, the angry members voted 77-32 to demolish the office extension. When the result of the vote became known, the Company Chairman, W Gordon (V16) and (known as the poison dwarf), Company Secretary Jimmy Neilson (V42) and Jimmy Dickson, garage manager (V76) all resigned. If they thought that their actions would sway the membership to change their vote, they were very much mistaken.

In what was viewed by some members of the committee as the downside of having facilities at the garage, plus the rule that members must purchase all their fuel there, meant that members would be at the garage every day. They would have access to the office bearers and ask questions or be able to get a grievance off their chest directly to the chairman or company secretary. The then chairman Jimmy Spowart, (half share V7) would have preferred being at Atholl Place, where he was more isolated from the members and he persuaded the Council to hold an Extraordinary General Meeting on 18th. September 1996.The item on the agenda was the proposal to sell off the filling station at East London Street. It became obvious at the meeting that the committee wished to sell up and convinced the membership that this was in their (the members) best interests and that the committee would look for other premises. A vote was taken, and the proposal was carried by 63 votes to 49. Spowart gave an undertaking that the Council would endeavour to find new premises with facilities for members. Members of the committee, John Lowe (V27) and Kenny Clyne (V149) later admitted it was a big mistake selling East London Street as the heart went out of the company.

The filling station was sold for £217,000 and as Spowart said after the sale went through "We were lucky to get rid of it." As God had stopped making land a long time ago and this was a city centre property at the start of a property boom his judgement must be called into question. A half-hearted attempt was made to secure other premises, but with Spowart less than enthusiastic, it was never going to happen. Any suggestions made to him were met with the response "I don't think that's suitable."

Only one site was discussed with the membership. In 1998, a retail unit with limited parking on Anderson Place was proposed but was rejected by the members as being unsuitable. This was the only premises offered to the members and Spowart had achieved his objective. He could avoid the members and would not have to answer questions on his running of the company on a daily basis. This was probably the worst time in the company's history, with a vast amount of the membership losing faith in the committee. It was time for Sir Basil of Currie (W.O. Smith V128) to mount his white charger again and come to the rescue of the company as he had done on numerous other occasions.

Surviving a financial crisis in 1980, the committee comprising of Willie Dickson (V68 &V109) and W.O. Smith (V128) decided that the company be put on a more sound financial basis and so the decision was made to surcharge the members £115 in order that the company purchase the radio equipment outright instead of renting. Another important measure was convincing the older members of the committee, such as Dougie Logan (V12) that the office premises on Morrison Street were inadequate for the development of the company. A search was started for a suitable site and an offer was made for premises on Russell Road, but due to legal problems with the lease, the offer was withdrawn. When the premises at Atholl Place were offered, they were found to be suitable and Willie Smith and Willie Dickson set out to convince the committee that the purchase of Atholl Place for the sum of £35,500 was a step forward for the company. They prevailed and in 1982 the control room was moved from Morrison Street to Atholl

Place. The premises at 155 Morrison Street were sold for £7000.

In 1988, with the growing number of radio jobs passing through the control room and the slow procedure for dispatching them, Willie Smith began looking at alternative ways of dispatching work. As this was in the early days of data dispatch, his vision was not understood by a section of the membership.

At a meeting in 1989, members of the committee were given permission to visit Vancouver and check out MDI and visit control rooms of cab companies operating with the system. On their return and after much discussion in the "Howf," a meeting was held on 2nd. August 1989 where it was decided to award the contract to supply a data system to Phillips.

This was to be installed in three phases, but difficulties in introducing phase two, owing to software problems, and Phillips unable to meet the installation deadline, led to a meeting at Heriot Watt University in 1991 where the membership voted to cancel the contract with Phillips and seek compensation. Four other data companies offered systems and it was finally decided to go with the Auriega System.

After meeting with the District Council and the veiled threat to increase the number of licenses issued, the company decided to open up the stations on a three month trial basis. This proved successful and a meeting was held with British Rail to terminate the franchise in 1978.

Radio Cabs / Comcab

The Company was formally started on 14th. November 1952, when a group of cabbies realizing the potential benefit of having a two-way radio in the cab decided to leave the Edinburgh Taxi Owners Association.

Their views were at variance with the majority of members of the Association who would prevaricate for another six years.

They opened premises on West Crosscauseway before moving to the Upper Bow. Unlike the other radio companies, which are co-operatives with members having a share in the company, Radio Cabs was run by directors and were seen by the trade as laid back with little or no discipline. The management never got involved in the politics of the trade preferring to keep a low profile.

In March 2002, the directors of Capital Castle Cabs sold out to Comcab and in 2004 Comcab made overtures to buy City Cabs but were turned down. They made a tenuous offer again in 2010 when merger talks between City and Central again were put on the agenda.

Directors were, Angus Tyler, Dougie Grubb, Henry Wilson and Mrs. Elliot, who since the death of her husband, ran Pettigrews garage on Jordan Lane.

Radio Cabs, whose offices in Upper Bow were bought out by Alan Napier, Rab Veitch, Bobby Clark and Ian Banks in April 1990 and sold out to Comcab in April 2000.Radio Cabs were dissolved on 26th April 2004 and closed their offices at Stewart House, Eskmill Business Park, Musselburgh. They moved to Spitfire House, Turnhouse Road.

Comcab ceased operations in 2017 when they merged with Central Radio Taxis.

In 1998, Rab Veitch started an offshoot called Radio Taxi Services (RTS) fitting radios and meters in premises in Porteous Pend. He merged with Adam Fraser who operated Radio Technology Services (RTS) in Mayfield. Due to expansion, they rebranded to Cabcom and moved to New Lairdship Yards, this being convenient for the cab office. They became agents for Halda, and Aquila meters. In 2001 they became the agents for Digitax meters. Rab Veitch sold out to Doug Hope in 2013 and retired but still kept his connection to the trade by continuing to organize the food at the kids outing, a job he has done for over 30 years.

Central Radio Taxis

Founder members of Central Radio Taxis 50th. anniversary 2018 George Frost,Peter Haynes,Eric Tice,Charlie Dickson,Archie McCall,Alex Webster missing Bill Blanche

Central Radio Taxis

In 1968, a group of licensed taxi owners were dissatisfied with the working practises of the existing companies, such as City Cabs, Radio Cabs and George Hall taxis, who were based at the West End and only operated a day shift with the office closing at 6pm.

Therefore a nucleus of the existing Motor Hirers Association (M.H.A.) decided to establish their own company where they could control their own destiny. A meeting was held on the 12th. of May 1968 at Ruskin House, Windsor Street, Edinburgh, with 31 potential members attending. Mr. J. Archer, after being voted interim Chairman, proposed the dissolving of the M.H.A. and that its Committee should serve on the board of the new company which was to be called Central Radio Taxis. (CRT)

Six men were so committed to the new venture that they put up their houses as guarantee.

At the same meeting, it was also agreed that corporate signage should be designed, and a radio call sign agreed. The badge, a two-inch square with a yellow background and a blue flash in the centre was established. Suggestions for a call sign were made, such as Dixie and X Ray. Victor was ruled out as City Cabs already used it. 'Peter' was agreed to as the new call sign. For identification purposes each cab was given a number prefixed with Peter. To distinguish between owners and drivers, the owners were given the colour blue and driver's or jockeys as they are known in the trade, had the colour red (e.g. owner calling control would say P15 blue.) Later call sign identifiers were used on windows in positions approved by the cab office. These were visible yellow numbers, to be easily seen by other drivers.

The Committee eventually found premises to rent at 131 Gilmore Place and an agreement with Pye Communication to install radio equipment was established.

2,000 hires were being covered per week, but the Committee felt more could be covered if the fleet would accept more radio work instead of opting for the street hire. This is a problem that still affects radio taxi companies up to the present time. However the Chairman appealed to the membership with the statement "Remember, this is no boardroom company, it belongs to us all, and we all have the same stake in our future prosperity." This statement is even more relevant today.

A rival company, Riddells of Braid Road, was bought over for £1000.00 due to the fact it held lucrative contracts in the south of the City. These included the Princess Margaret Rose Hospital on Frogston Road West, the City Hospital on Greeenbank Drive, Astlie Anslie Hospital on Canaan Lane, Craighouse Hospital on Craighouse Road and the Royal Edinburgh on Morningside Park. This was supplemented by a loyal customer base. The building which housed Riddles taxi office still stands on the railway bridge at Morningside station, now home to a roofing company.

By 1970, the membership was now 70 and job numbers

were rising exponentially, so new, larger premises were needed. In 1972, a proposal to purchase 131 and 133 Gilmore Place was rejected as they were too small, so 163 Gilmore Place was purchased on 4th. April 1972.This was to be Centrals home until 2016. The company continued to grow and membership expanded to 96 in 1976. In 2016 the Company sold its control room premises at 163 Gilmore Place, and administration premises at 12 St Peters Buildings, and bought new premises at 12 Bankhead Avenue, which included all its businesses in one modern space.

The joining fee would be increased to £7,000.00 then £8,000.00.

These positions were transferable by negotiation and approval by the company.

Using this system the fleet increased to 417 in 2008.After a takeover of Comcab, the number of members rose to 465, making it the largest taxi fleet in the city. Unfortunately around 2016, due to multiple PHC licenses being issued and smart phone technology available, black cab company positions have become less desirable, to now being almost worthless.

When a member was unable to work due to injury or ill health, it was the practice to "pass the hat around" to collect money to help them through trying times. The flaw in this scheme was that a well-known and popular person would get more than a less well known one. To prevent this from happening, the committee decided to establish a welfare fund with monthly donations from the members radio dues. This is administered voluntarily by a committee of members autonomously from the main Committee. It was thought this system was more equitable, rather than having to ask for donations. There are many members and drivers who have been appreciative of the Welfare Committee and the payments given in their time of need.

From its inception, CRTs workforce organized social events such as golf, football, and fishing clubs and participate in many charitable events, most notably the annual Edinburgh Taxi Trade Outing for disadvantaged children.

Due to increased competition from competitors, it was decided to change the company's image. This was done with the introduction of corporate work wear. This did much to improve the company profile and is much appreciated by their customers.

With the Company expanding over time, the need to replace the outdated radio system with new technology to keep up with competitors was imperative. CRT, it might be argued by some, was a little reluctant to embrace new technology, but eventually utilized computer technology with the Auriga system, and later smart phone technology with the Cordic system.

Several approaches have been made to discuss the two associations merging, indeed, it would seem to make perfect sense. Less costs for staff wages, premises, administration, systems and management. Unfortunately, old disputes over discounts for customers, railway station permits, CEC negotiations and historical perceived grievances could not be overcome. This was coupled with the fact that members of the management teams were reluctant to give up their grip on power. It was therefore a surprise when the Airport authorities approached both Associations to jointly serve the lucrative airport rank, in conjunction with a private hire company. It must be said, this was after many years of aggressive lobbying by a large number of Edinburgh taxi drivers and long-suffering airport taxi users. The airport management argued that they wanted a greater choice of vehicles for taxi customers.

A joint venture between City Cabs and Central called 'Forward Travel' was created on 31st October 2007 and it gained the contract to operate at the airport. The new company was very successful with drivers from both companies working together and a lot of the perceived grievances melted away. This went on until the Airport management wanted to contract only one company to serve their taxi customers along with a PHC company. City Cabs was chosen, thus ending the miracle of the merge. When the contract was up for renewal in 2014, Forward Travel was not invited to tender. It was decided that each company should tender alone, which suited the airport, as the two companies would be outbidding each other. There could only be one winner and it was not the taxi trade. City Cabs won the contract and Forward Travel was disbanded. EHPC entered into a joint venture with City Cabs to operate the contract and many of the drivers in Onward Travel decided to join EHPC. As a result, the airport remains a bone of contention in the trade. When the tender came up for renewal in 2018, Central's bid included installing electric charging points and offering electric cars as private hire vehicles and the new TXE taxi, plus an electronic way for passengers to book a cab in advance, but their bid was not successful as it appeared that the airport was only interested in what they could collect from barrier charges.

Due to a request from CEC, the Taxicard scheme which serves wheelchair and special needs users with discounts, was shared by both associations but was administered by one company to cut costs. CRT won the contract.

This included a need for several saloon cars with PHC licenses to accommodate a choice of vehicles. A number of Nissan Leafs were purchased to cover the Lothian Health Board contract along with the Taxi-card scheme and Central went into an arrangement with Persevere private hire. Ironically this is something the membership argued against for much of its existence, on the basis that it was a black cab company and nothing else, probably missing out many business opportunities. Due to the arrival of the Nissan Leaf and the new TXE, Central were the first to install charging points at Bankhead

Throughout its history, CRT has seen its rival black cab companies as its main competitors, but gradually over time PHC companies have aggressively moved into the taxi market by offering large discounts due to their lower costs. This coupled with the use of smart phone technology appealed to younger customers.

With no upper limit on the number of PHC licenses in 2020, it is now 3,000 and rising. The Council seem unwilling to address this through a survey of over provision. It seems strange since there is a cap on black cab numbers. With CEC enacting a zero emissions policy for the city, and insisting the taxi trade be at the forefront, it is going to take a great commitment from license taxi owners to purchase a new electric black cab costing over £55,000.

Central Radio Taxis has been in existence for over 50 years and has moved with the times, sometimes reluctantly, but with 465 members, it remains strong with a loyal customer base and many large company contracts to help it survive.

Airport

Since the opening of the new terminal building in 1977, the provision of taxis or PHC to cover the work has been a contentious one and even today the wrangling continues. A report in the Evening News, in January 2000, stated Edinburgh Airport wants to scrap its controversial fleet of taxis and replace them with private mini cabs, it was claimed today. The move could mean lower fares for passengers, but longer travel times between the airport and the city.

The Airport authorities say that the idea is only an option - but the city's former head of licensing said she was told about the plan ten months ago and was asked to keep quiet about it.

The news came as the city council's licensing committee itself vote to get rid of airport taxis, whose 107 saloon car and people carriers currently monopolize trade, in return for permits. The change would allow Edinburgh's traditional black cabs, which are slightly cheaper, to move in on the airport, while airport drivers would be allowed to operate black cabs in return.

In 1984, the council decided to create airport taxis, so 60 were created from existing PHC vehicles. The PHC vehicles were all saloon or estate and all white. They were not fitted with meters; the fare being calculated on odometer readings as it was a fixed mileage charge. The charge was 15% more than the licensed trade. This was justified as the airport cabs had to return to the airport empty. All jobs were calculated this way, unlike the licensed taxis who, on country jobs, added 50% of the metered fare. This arrangement ceased when the airport taxis had radios fitted allowing them to get return work.

By 2000, the council decided to do away with airport taxis and all were given an Edinburgh taxi license. This meant that some operators who had PHC licenses had to sit the topographical test. Many of the drivers given an Edinburgh license, sold it and purchased a PHC license at the airport.

The operators formed a company, Onward Travel in 2004, under the umbrella of Comcab using private cars. Onward Travel was dissolved in 2019, with some of its drivers opting to join EHPC.

Civic Code

One of the biggest disasters to affect the taxi trade nationwide was the Civic Government Act (Scotland) in 1982. The local elections of 1984 saw Labour, under leader Alec Wood, win 34 out of 62 seats and for the first time take control of the City. The new administration's first act of power was to fly the red flag over the City Chambers. This was a sign of things to come. The new council was definitely left wing and more than one councillor stated that they would finish the taxi trade and the "fat cats" who were the operators. Eleanor McLaughlin stated that there were too many taxis parked outside 'big fancy homes.' She failed to understand that taxi driving is a second profession for some and that many owners had been successful business men in other areas before becoming taxi drivers and that these were men and women who had put up a substantial amount of money to invest in the transport infrastructure.

The act introduced by the Conservative government, but implemented by a Labour council, made taxi licenses non-transferable. At the stroke of a pen, license holders lost their investment, which many probably would use as a retirement pension. One person unfortunately purchased a license and taxi cab with a radio position in CRT, but two days later the Civic Code was enacted. It is thought the license portion of the deal was £10,000. Now lost!

Under the new act many people took the opportunity to apply for a license from CEC and license numbers rose sharply.

When the Act was introduced, the Council decided to put new issue taxi licenses on at the rate of 10 a month. This strategy worked well as it gave the cab office time to allocate test dates and it also gave prospective owners a chance to put financial arrangements in place.

The recognized requirement was a new vehicle, or one no older than one year.

This was challenged by Graham Murray, who after studying the licensing conditions, found there was no requirement to put on a new vehicle, it was the cab inspectors personal opinion. The case went to court and Murray won when the Council admitted he was correct. This led to some people putting on older cabs as they could not get the finance for a new vehicle. Many people took up the offer of a new issue plate as it did not have the same financial burden. This was seen by existing owners as a threat to their livelihoods and Graham Murray was treated like a pariah by some members of the trade. Ironically after winning the right to put on an older cab, one year later Graham purchased a new cab.

CRT planned to protect and expand their investment and allow more license holders to become members. There would be for a joining fee of £5,000.00 to be paid up over a period of a few years. This saw the fleet increase to 200 in

1995. Alec Graham, secretary of the Edinburgh Taxi Owners Association (ETOA) discovered a potential loophole in the legislation and sought legal advice. Later it was negotiated with the CEC that licenses could be transferred between incorporated Companies or Partnerships, this would greatly assist the Edinburgh taxi trade.

Chapter 8

Controllers

Linda Muir who was one of the best controllers in the trade, was appointed City Cabs office manageress in 1983. She held this position until her retirement in 2008, when she became responsible for the training of new control room staff on a part time basis. Any driver who worked with Linda will remember her unique style of dispatching work, especially in the centre of town on a busy Friday and Saturday night, when she would ask over the air for a quote from the West End to Glasgow. After a space of a few minutes she would request cars for the West End.

There were two types of driver who would bid for this work, 'The needy and the greedy.' When they were given jobs at hotels and pubs in the West End, and no job with a Glasgow destination being dispatched, Linda, on being asked, where was the Glasgow job, her reply was always "They decided not to go." She employed this tactic on numerous occasions much to the amusement of the regular night shift cabbies.

Madge Dickson was a controller for 34 years until she retired in 1995.

Anyone who worked night shift during the 1970's and 80's would have had the pleasure of working with Jackie Robertson and Vic McLean. The original odd couple, they were complete opposites in everything. He looked like Popeye's arch enemy Bluto, often with a fish supper in the inside pocket of his jacket, and she dressed thirty years younger than her age, and with all the airs and graces of a lady. Many a cabbie was on the receiving end of her acerbic wit and ten minutes later, when the penny dropped, would think of a suitable reply. Jackie was proud of the fact she was the first go-go dancer in Edinburgh, performing in the Canny Mans bar.

Sometimes sharing a flat, but more often a table in a bar, they had their own unique way of dispatching work. The regular drivers knew how they worked, and worked with them, but it took a bit of getting used to. Good advice given to new drivers was "Work with Jackie and Vic and you will make money." However, with the coming of data dispatch, they were unable to adjust to the changes and so two of the most popular characters left the company.

Working one Hogmanay, I received six cans of Export from a fare for my New Year but got fed up with them rolling around the luggage compartment. I picked up a job from the Caledonian Hotel to Corstorphine, I called in on the radio and told Vic that I would be passing the office in a minute and if he was at the door, he would get something. Handing over the six pack I continued on my way but had only reached Haymarket when Jackie called me asking where her drink was. I told her that there were 3 for each of them. She informed me that Vic had drunk five whilst walking up the stair.

Jackie wrote a collection of stories from life called "With Foot in Mouth" in which she relates the time she and Vic were guests at a wedding reception and were seated at a table beside the Irish priest who had officiated at the ceremony. The conversation was stilted and convoluted. When Vic asked the priest what he would like to drink "Ah! Do you think they'll have a Britvic?" The conversation being as strained as it was, Vic naturally thought that the priest was addressing him by name and promptly asked the barmaid "Do you have any Brit?"

On dispatching a job from the Council housing department to the Royal Infirmary, Vic quipped "Probably had a heart attack when he found out how much his rent will be."

His favourite expression when dealing with cabbies was "Dearie, Dearie Me!" followed by a verbal put-down ending further conversation.

One night, when taking a fare home at 1am, the passenger asked me if I could book him a cab for 6am. to go to the airport. Passing the order to Vic, he asked me if the fare was still in the cab. When I replied yes, he told me to turn the volume up on the radio as he wanted a word with him. He then launched into a tirade as to how he should have been in bed ages ago and he better not keep the driver waiting as we did not operate a wake-up service. He put the fear of God into the young man who sat in the back of the cab with eyes wide in horror, nodding vigorously in agreement before running indoors. I think it's safe to assume he did not sleep that night.

Each radio company had this type of controller. Radio Cabs had Jack Harkins who entertained the night shift with renditions on the violin. Central, with Helen Hogg, who called work to the beat of popular tunes and John Weir who was known for his sense of humour. A favourite with him was on 1st. April. He would call a job picking up at the Zoo and the passengers name was Mr. Lyons. Every year some gullible cabbie fell for it much to the amusement of the rest of the fleet. Working night shift, he would switch off all the lights and lock the office door. When the day shift arrived, they would be met with locked, darkened premises. A note on the door would inform them that as it had been a quiet night, he had locked up and gone home and that the keys for the office were in the all-night bakers shop across the road. The day shift controller would get in a panic as she knew that there were a lot of 6 o'clock orders to be dispatched and would run across the road and ask the baker for the keys, only to be met with a blank look. Running back to the office, she would see the night shift peeking through the window blinds. It was with some sadness that the driver's embraced data dispatch, knowing that we will never hear this type of controller again.

John, Jimmy and Charlie Weir were three brothers who came into the cab trade from the undertaking profession and none of them fitted the stereotypical image of an undertaker. All had a wicked sense of humour and were always ready with a joke. John and Jimmy were in Central Radio Taxis while Charlie was in City Cabs.

Charlie was for many years chairman of the Edinburgh Taxi Trade Handicapped Children's Outing. When going around the ranks selling immune badges or raffle books, it was a brave cabbie who refused to buy and when he asked if the cab was going on the outing he would not take no for an answer.

On one occasion, when I informed him in 1980, that I was returning from holiday and arriving at Glasgow Airport at 3am, he said "No problem. You don't pick the kids up until 9am. "I'll just put your name down."

His sense of humour was on the black side and I was never quite sure if some of the stories he relayed about the time he was an undertaker were true.

One of his favourite stories concerned the laying out of a body and discovering that the man had worn a wig. His wife was most insistent that he should look as normal as possible, but there was a problem with the wig, as it kept slipping off. "Easy solved" he said. "We just used a carpet tack and combed the hair over it."

Another was of a woman who told him that as her husband, who had just died, was the best husband in the world and that nothing was too good for him. She wanted him laid out in the finest of suits and could Charlie possibly arrange it. After the funeral the woman said she was most impressed with the Savile Row suit her husband had been wearing. She then asked Charlie how much her bill was. Charlie explained that the next body in was that of a wealthy businessman wearing a new Savile Row suit. Charlie then asked the man's new widow if she wanted her husband buried in his Savile Row suit, to which she replied, "He was an absolute bastard and I don't give a toss what he wears. I am just glad to see the back of him." Charlie then explained to the grieving widow, that in an attempt to save her money, he employed an old undertaker's trick. "What did you do?" she enquired, "Did you swap the suits?" "No" he answered, "The heads."

Having survived his two brothers, sadly Charlie died in March 2010.

Chapter 9

Main Dealers

Mann And Overton

1912 Unic Taxi
Photo Courtesy
Anthony Blackman

In 1896, Tom Overton went to study in Paris where he met J.J. Mann and they set up a business importing cars. Mann stayed in Paris, whilst Overton returned to London. He saw how quickly cars were replacing horses and cashed in on the boom.

By 1904, just over 6,000 cabs had been licensed in London, a tremendous achievement when almost every other form of transport was horse drawn.

1907 saw them importing the Unic from France and modifying the Chassis to meet the Metropolitan Conditions of Fitness (C.o.F) which came into force in 1906, part of which was the 25ft. turning circle. This proved to be more reliable and better suited to the Hackney trade than the Renault and other competitors which had up until then, a clear field.

After a long illness J.J. Mann died in 1908 and Tom Overton continued to run the business himself until 1916, when his brother William joined the company. Tom's son Robert joined the company in 1930. After the Second World War, Tom Overton decided to move into the property market and William ran the company.

By the late 1920's, import duties made imported cabs too expensive and as they were now outdated, William started looking for a suitable replacement.

The Austin Heavy 12/4 was giving good service as a taxi in the provinces, so William altered the chassis in their workshop to meet with the C.o.F.

Having gained approval, he tried to arrange a meeting with Herbert Austin, but Austin would not see him. Refusing to take no as a final answer, he took a seat outside Austin's office and declared to his secretary "I will wait here until he does." At the end of the days business, as Austin was leaving the office, he saw Overton sitting in the waiting room. "Why are you still here?" enquired Austin, to which Overton replied "I will sit here every day until you agree to a meeting as I wish to order 500 chassis." Austin acquiesced to his request and supplied the modified chassis. The Austin cab went on sale in 1930 and due to its reliability and price, within a year it was the best-selling cab in London and by 1935 would have sales reaching 1,200.

Mann and Overton would build on this success and go on to dominate the taxi market in London.

Following a decision by London Taxis International to dispense with dealer franchises throughout Britain, Mann and Overton opened up a showroom and workshop in Broxburn in 2010, but this was to be a short lived.

Chapter 10

Vehicles

The meeting between Herbert Austin and William Overton would herald a new era in the taxi trade in Britain. The Austin 12/4 High Lot, so known as it was higher than its competitors, quickly became a favourite with the cab trade and was soon outselling its rivals, Beardmore and the Morris Oxford. Priced at £395, more than seven hundred were sold between 1930 and 1932.The new model introduced in 1934 was known as Austin 12/4 Low Loader and would give great service until 1946.

The Austin 12/4 Low Loader brochure for 1938 stated that:

The price of cab, complete with luxuriously upholstered standard cab landaulets body, cellulose blue with full windscreen and including front and rear bumpers, fire extinguisher, horn, number plates, license holder, taxi roof sign, trico visional wiper and speedometer. All exterior fittings are chrome plated.

List price £395

Hire purchase terms were Deposit £50, with monthly repayments of £10, making a total price £472

You would receive an £18 bonus if the purchase was completed in 40 months, and the bonus reduced by £3 for each month exceeding the above mentioned.

1937 Austin 12/4 Low Loader

At the outbreak of war Austin stopped delivery of the 12/4 chassis to Mann and Overton as they were required for military vehicles.

The Nuffield Group, makers of the Morris Oxford cab had a prototype model in 1940 but it did not pass the C.o.F. until 1946 and going into production in 1947.

It was sold by the Beardmore dealership to a desperate London cab trade.

The London cab trade had taken a severe beating during the Second World War with a large number of cabs destroyed in the Blitz and many more converted as auxiliary fire engines with ladders on the roof and towing a water bowser. They were not very effective, but as the drivers were cabbies, they could get to fires faster than the fire brigade as many roads were blocked with bomb damage and they always knew the quickest alternative route.

After the war William Overton realized that they needed a new vehicle to compete with the Morris Oxford and where they had been market leaders, they were now behind their competitors. Drastic action had to be taken and quickly, if they were to survive.

In 1946 Austin, who gave all their models a code number e.g. A, AB, ACD delivered a new chassis to Mann and Overton, and as it was for a taxi, they gave it the code number FX. The chassis needed alterations and when it was returned to Mann and Overton, it was longer and stronger and designated FX2. The new chassis was submitted to the public carriage office and passed the C.o.F. in March 1947.

With the new chassis Mann and Overton needed to find someone who could build the body. Pre-war, the bodies had been coach built, but that was now too expensive.

Austin were not interested as they had no spare production space due to the introduction of new models and were not interested in production numbers of around 15 per week.

Austin management, who had worked with Carbodies during the war, introduced Robert Overton to Ernest Jones and Jack Orr.

After discussions, it was decided that Carbodies could produce an all steel body at a realistic price in the small numbers required by Mann and Overton. As a result a deal was struck whereby Austin would supply chassis to Carbodies who would build, paint and fit out the cabs while Mann and Overton would sell them exclusively in London, while Austin would sell them elsewhere in Britain.

The initial development costs and all future modifications were split on a three-way basis, Mann and Overton would provide 50% of the money while Austin and Carbodies would provide 25% each.

At a meeting between Carbodies Jack Orr and Ernest Jones, Robert Overton and the P.C.O., the design of the body was discussed and the P.C.O. demanded design changes that included, the roof sign be made smaller and for passenger privacy, darkened glass was to be used in the rear window and no interior rear-view mirror would be allowed. The P.C.O. could not decide which shade of yellow should be used for the hire sign glass and after looking at different samples, one was chosen, but only after three weeks.

The FX2 gained type approval in June 1947 but in October of that year Austin decided that it would be uneconomical to produce the small numbers of the 14hp engine that was to be fitted into the taxi as they had decided to fit a bigger engine in the A70, so the new 2.2 litre engine was fitted in the FX2 in 1948. With the new roof sign, new engine and other design changes the cab gained a new model number FX3.

Austin FX 3
photo courtesy of Dave Taylor

Mann and Overton were having cash flow problems as the London taxi trade were not buying new cabs and were cutting back on servicing, so they were slow to come up with the cash needed to manufacture the numbers needed. After two and a half years in production the FX3 was introduced to the London cab trade.

On 11th. June 1948, with two London fleet garages taking one prototype each, Central Autos took JXN 842 and W.H. Cook took JXN 841.

The FX3 finally took to the streets in November 1948. For the first time, the driver was enclosed with a glass panel on his left. A severe financial blow struck the FX3 in 1951 when double purchase tax was levied, pushing the price of a new cab up to over £1,100. A diesel engine version came into production in 1953, and although costing an additional £85, plus tax, it immediately became a success as Derv was a fraction of the price of petrol. Another bonus was after strong lobbying, purchase tax on taxis was abolished. Sales of the FX3 were helped in 1953 when Austin and Morris Oxford merged to become the British Motor Corporation and as the FX3 was the newer model, it was decided to stop production of the Oxford.

Using a pressed steel body and running gear from the Austin sixteen, with a 2.2 litre (2199cc) engine, the one that would eventually be used in A70 Hereford and Hampshire models. The chassis was a pressed steel box section with all round leaf springs and Girling mechanical brakes. In 1951, a changeover to hydraulics all round took place. A four-speed gear box was fitted and a hand operated hydraulic jacking system operated by a lever applied to a pump mounted on the nearside of the chassis under the bonnet and worked fore and aft, either or both axles could be lifted simultaneously. The Standard Motor Company introduced an engine with a 2 litre capacity normally fitted in the Ferguson tractor. In 1953, London fleet owner Birch Brothers, offered a diesel conversion which cost £325, including labour. This move by Birch Brothers prompted Austin to develop their own 2.2 diesel engine in 1954, and the model was named FX3D and cost £95 more than the petrol version.

The FL1, was a four door hire car version, without the roof mounted hire light and bench front seat, which necessitated having a column gear change, were produced until 1958, when it was superseded by the FX4. In total 12,435 were produced, 7267 FX3's were licensed in London.

It was marketed as "The Austin Metropolitan Taxicab" and the price was £936.00

In the ten years between 1948-1958, over 13,737 FX3's were built, with an average of fifteen per week.

The 1957 price of a FX3 ex. works was petrol, £910 before tax, diesel £1012 before tax.

Austin FX4

Mann and Overton had planned the FX3 to have a production life of ten years, so in 1958 a new model, the FX4 was launched at a price of £1,198. This was the first cab to have four doors and despite many faults, the trade gradually came to accept it. Under the ten year production programme, Mann and Overton began planning a replacement in 1965. When Carbodies quoted £35,000 for a new body, they found this too expensive and it was decided to revamp the existing model. Finally rectifying many of the inherent faults, one of which was the water leak under the battery which caused rain water to pour onto the driver's right foot. Indeed, in wet weather, drivers would tie a plastic bag around their leg in an attempt to keep it dry. The second fault was the heater pipes for the passenger heater. They were situated under the rear seat, which ran along the chassis, making them virtually useless. They were moved into the driver's compartment and the heater to the bulkhead.

In 1973 Britain joined the Common Market and new European regulations governing Motor vehicles came into force in 1974, requiring all vehicles to be crash tested. Carbodies informed Mann and Overton that they could not afford to supply a vehicle to the Motor Industry Research Association as the vehicle would be a write off. Mann and Overton had no choice. If no cab was presented for the test, no more vehicles would be produced.

The test involved mounting the vehicle on a track and running it into a concrete wall at 30mph.

The car which was tested before the taxi was a Lamborghini and after impact, M.I.R.A. staff found the engine in the driver's compartment and stated it was one of the worst they had seen. When the taxi was examined after its test, the crash link was found to have collapsed, as intended, and the steering wheel was almost where it had been before the test. The only thing that had broken, was the partition glass and it had only moved 5/8 of an inch from where it had been before the test.

In their report, M.I.R.A. stated that the results were the best they had ever seen.

Mann and Overton's reluctance to spend any money on improving the cab was causing frustration at Carbodies, their attitude being, why spend money on changes that they were not required to make under the C.O.F.? An example of this was to refuse two speed wipers on the grounds that cabs in London, owing to traffic, did not travel very fast and so were not needed. Also, they would not pay for a servo braking system all round, only on the front wheels. This was despite advice from motor engineers that it would cause problems when braking. It was also felt that they were not passing on driver's complaints but were filtering them to suit their own ends. Eventually Carbodies decided to go it alone and develop a completely new cab independently of Mann and Overton. This would free them from the financial restraints that Mann & Overton imposed, and the cab was to be called FX5.

In the nine years between 1971 and 1980, inflation had pushed the price of a new cab up from £1,200 to £7,000

Carbodies long time General Manager Bill Lucas, retired in 1979 due to ill health. His successor Grant Lockart decided to scrap the FX5 and build one based on the Range Rover that was to be called CR6.

The name CR6 comes from City Rover and model number 6. It was the first wheelchair accessible cab to be built.

The front grille and headlights were restyled to avoid confusion, but Rover were not keen on having it used as a taxi as they thought that it would detract from the upper class market, they were targeting.

It was announced to the trade in 1982 and prototypes were trialled in different cities. In Edinburgh, Gus Tyler of Radio Cabs tested it for six months, but it was unreliable. Due to the testing of wheelchair access, the cab was running a year behind schedule and with Carbodies in serious financial difficulties, the project was scrapped.

When B.L. sold the Austin engine to India, the only available replacement was the 2.2 Land Rover. After a very short test time, it was fitted to the cab which became known as the FX4R, the "R" standing for Rover. It took to the road in November 1982 at an on the road price of £8,739. The result was a disaster. The engine was under powered, belched smoke and was prone to breakdowns. In the words of one cabbie unfortunate to have bought one "It would not pull a soldier off a whore." On the hills of Edinburgh it was a nightmare. When going uphill fully loaded, it had to be stopped to engage 1st. gear. The result was that the trade shunned it and very few people bought one through choice. On the plus side, it was the first cab to have power steering and servo brakes all round.

Manganese Bronze Holdings, who bought Mann and Overton, formed London Taxis International (LTI.) Introducing a new model, the FX4S in November 1985, the cab now had a new engine and new black steel bumpers. The on-road price was £11,239.

After a change in management at Carbodies the CR6 was scrapped in 1986.

In late 1987, the FX4S had a makeover including a new vinyl interior and it became the FX4S-Plus.

New legislation came into force in February 1989 which required all purpose-built cabs to have wheelchair accessibility.

Probably one of the best things to happen to the trade was the introduction of the "Fairway" in February 1989. The choice of name was a link with the past, as Bobby Jones had introduced it in 1933. Powered by a 2.7 Nissan TD27 diesel engine with a choice of four speed automatic or five speed gearbox it was quiet, smooth, economical, fast and very reliable. The trade loved it and soon there was a waiting list to purchase as the factory could not produce them fast enough to meet the demand. Many owners who had held on to their cabs rather than upgrade to the hated FX4R, now queued up to buy.

It was probably too reliable as drivers held on to them for longer periods and it was not unknown for some cabs to clock up more than 500,000 trouble free miles. The interior was the same vinyl as the FX4S-Plus, but it now came with a sliding sunroof and was available in a choice of spec, Bronze, Silver and Gold, prices started at £14,274 for a bronze manual rising to £16,750 for the Gold automatic.

In the first year of production it broke all records with sales well over 3,000.

LTI kept improving the cab, such as the brakes which were basically the same as when the FX4 was launched in 1958, but with the addition of a swivel seat and low step to aid the less mobile and red coloured door handles and seat panels to aid the partially sighted. Named the Fairway Driver, it was launched in 1992. Further modifications were made to the next model, the Fairway Driver Plus and in 1995 the Fairway 95 had a split rear seat to allow easier wheelchair access.

This was to be the last model as LTI were planning a new model, the TXI to be launched in October 1997 and so came to an end almost fifty years continuous production of the FX4.

The last Fairway off the production line in October 1997, was given the registration number R1 PFX (RIP FX) and was presented to the motor museum at Beaulieu in Hampshire.

Edinburgh Council decided that the Fairway would no longer be licensed after 2002. In London, the trade was given a ten-year exemption which ended in 2012. Many London cabs when they came "off the plate" were snapped up by enthusiasts from all over the world proving that its status as an icon was deserved.

The FX 3 and later the FX 4 were versatile vehicles with some being converted into newspaper delivery vans, some into hearses and others into pick-ups.

New model - new name, TXI comes from the word taxi with the A missing. Stylish new lines and powered by a Nissan engine, it was the first taxi that did not rattle, squeak, leak or have draughts. During the first year its sales broke all records with many being sold abroad. However, new smoke emission levels were being introduced and the Nissan engine would not comply.

LTI were running out of time to get a new engine in place and opted for the Ford Duratorq turbo diesel. The new model named the TXII was launched in February 2002 and because of the short development time, the engine proved a disaster. Problems with the timing chain and drive line went unresolved for a long time and the main dealer just shrugged their shoulders and offered the excuse "They are all like that" and once again the trades confidence in a vehicle plummeted

A new engine was required and quickly, as there were other competitors on the scene and so the TX4 was launched in February 2007 with an engine from VM Motori of Italy. The engine was a success, but problems arose with the radiators and it became a source of bragging rights as to who had the most replacements. But there was trouble looming as there were fires breaking out under the bonnet and all vehicles between certain chassis numbers were ordered off the road until modifications could be made.

On the 15th. September 1998, Robert Grieve at the Taxi Examination Centre, received a phone call from Alec Lothian about his TX4 going on fire.

He telephoned John Paton's to see if they knew anything about this and he was told that there was no cause for concern as the work that was required was to be done when the vehicles came in for service.

After discussing this with the Licensing Department of the council and LTI being unable to assure the cab inspector that there was no risk of the affected vehicles going on fire, the decision was made to prohibit (red label) the vehicles from chassis number 200001 - 20100, 67 in total for Edinburgh. It was a sad day to see all these vehicles going in to the Taxi Examination Centre on Murrayburn Road, to be put off the road for an indeterminate time.

It took a long time to identify what the problem was and a whole range of work had to be carried out involving removal of the engine and gearbox. This was a long job and would take approximately 12 hours to complete.

Due to the length of time it was taking to fix the problem, it was decided to fit a fire extinguisher kit. In the event of a vehicle going on fire, it would be extinguished immediately, this was a temporary fix until the full work could be completed. This work would take an hour or two to complete.

So by the 21st of October all vehicles were back on the road.

This sad affair rumbled on for a long time as owners pursued compensation for being off the road for up to 6 weeks.

William Beardmore and Company was a Scottish engineering and shipbuilding company based in Glasgow. As well as shipbuilding, the company made railway engines and aeroplanes. At the end of the first World War the company started to make cars and taxis. William Beardmore sponsored Ernest Shackleton on his Antarctic expedition, who in gratitude named the Beardmore glacier in his name.

Production of the Beardmore Taxi began at Paisley in 1919 with what became known as the Mk1. This was designed to meet the Conditions of Fitness for London Taxis. It was a very tough and reliable vehicle and it earned itself the name of "The Rolls-Royce of taxicabs." Beardmore was the first to introduce a new type of taxi cab and by the mid 1920's claimed half of the London taxi market. Following the removal of William Beardmore from the board of his company in 1929, Beardmore Motors was bought out by its directors, and taxi production was moved from Scotland to Hendon. Here in 1932 a new model, the Mk4 Paramount was introduced,

After the Second World War, Beardmore Motors sold and serviced the new Nuffield Oxford cab.

Nuffield Oxford Cab

However, after British Motor Company (B.M.C.) axed the model in favour of their own model the FX3, Beardmore Motors then returned to making their own cabs. The model they introduced in 1954, was the Mk7 Paramount, which had a traditional style coach-built body of aluminium panels over an ash frame, built by Windover. The engine was from a Mk1 Ford Consul (later, a Mk2 Consul) and finally a Ford Zephyr. It would have a short production life as it was ended in late 1966. Final production of the Mk7 amounted to just over 650 cabs.

1966 Mark 7 Beardmore Taxi
Known Affectionately As "A Beardie"
Owners
Brian Fleming. Central Radio Taxis. Murray Fleming. Bob McCulloch.

This model was built between 1966 and 1967 and has the unusual feature of aluminium panels and glass fibre wings. Early Beardmore's were built in Glasgow at the end of World War 1 and continued until 1930, when production was moved to Hendon and finally ceased in 1969.

This particular model was originally registered in London on 28th June 1966 and worked there until 1970, when it was brought to Edinburgh and worked a further three years until the demise of the owner.

Brian Fleming bought it as a project that failed to materialize and lay in his garage until 1994. Being a member of Central Radio Taxis, Brian offered it to the company on indefinite loan as a publicity vehicle. The members of the company created a fund to enable it to be restored to its former glory. This was done to show the public how much the taxi of today has progressed with power steering, disc brakes, electronic meter and wheel chair capabilities.

Murray Fleming acquired the vehicle as a restoration project but due to work commitments was unable to carry this out and it lay unused for five years. The present owner acquired it in 2007 and carried out the long awaited restoration.

Metrocab

From 1958, Beardmore taxi bodies were made by coach and bus builder Weymann Motor Bodies. In 1963 /64 Metro-Cammell bought out Weymann.

From 1966 on, the Metropolitan Cammell Weymann name was dropped and only the abbreviated MCW title used.

Beardmore taxi production stopped in 1967, the Beardmore company itself going to the wall shortly thereafter. However, the link with taxi production was to survive through key staff working at MCW. They had begun design and development work for a new taxi cab – originally named the Metro-Beardmore – but with the demise of Beardmore, MCW took on the project, which duly became the MCW Metrocab taxi by the time of its launch.

With the cab trade increasingly disgruntled over LTI's virtual monopoly in London and its failure to come up with a new model to replace the ageing FX4, there was considerable interest in the potential for a choice of taxi at long last. For many, the Metrocab taxi appeared to fit the bill. Sporting a modern-looking shape, the first Metrocab taxi offered a Perkins diesel engine. In a major innovation, the new taxi cab had an all fibreglass body. This made the Metrocab both light and therefore economical to run and also rust-proof – answering a key sore point on the dominant Carbodies FX4 taxi cab. But reluctance to invest in further development of the cab, Metrocab production ceased and the whole taxi project was shelved.

During the early 1980's, Geoff Chater, a taxi engineer from Carbodies (later LTI), joined MCW and worked to recreate the Metrocab taxi concept and after almost two decades of LTI's virtual taxi monopoly, the Metrocab was re-launched in May 1987.

Metrocab was the first wheelchair accessible taxi, in anticipation of coming legislation. Because of its body being made of fibre glass, it quickly earned the nickname "a Tupperware cab."

In 1989 however, MCW's parent company, now named the Laird Group, ran into difficulties, which forced it to divest its train, bus and taxi-making interests. These were sold off separately, with the Metrocab taxi name and design being acquired by another West Midland's firm, Reliant.

Best known for their three-wheeler cars and vans as used by Del Boy in TV programme "Only Fools and Horses." Reliant also made the fibreglass bodies for the MCW Metrocab taxi and now moved full Metrocab production to its factory at Tamworth.

Other commercial troubles forced Reliant to sell off the Metrocab taxi business in 1991 to Hooper, a London coachbuilder who breathed new impetus into development of the Metrocab taxi, with important improvements, such as the first disc brakes featured on a purpose-built UK hackney cab. 1995 saw the launch of the Series II Metrocab taxi, with several cosmetic design enhancements and 1997 brought the Series III Metrocab taxi, which even provided electric windows for the cab driver. Six and even seven seat versions provided further revolution for the cab trade and helped attract growing taxi sales volumes. For many Metrocab fans the 'triple T' model, launched in 2000, represents the finest Metrocab taxi.

In part it was born out of necessity, as new Euro 3 emissions regulations forced a change from the original Ford Transit engine. Metrocab turned to Japan and fitted the TTT taxi with a 2.4L turbo-diesel from Toyota. However, the investment pressure to develop the next generation of Metrocab taxi, together with the London taxi market dominance of LTI and strong new provincial competition from modern-style taxis like the Peugeot Euro 7, caused Metrocab to struggle to reach minimum taxi sales volumes to keep the business viable. Metrocab went into administration and ceased taxi sales and production in 2003.New owners, KamKorp, reinstated production for a short time in 2005, before the factory gates shut for the last time.

John Paton & Son

When Ronnie Young's garage on Bonnington Road closed, anyone wishing to purchase a new vehicle had to travel to

Glasgow and also had to make the journey for servicing and repairs. To alleviate the problem, John Paton opened up premises in Lochrin Place in 1986. The premises were soon found to be too small and they moved to Dunedin Street, before withdrawing from the taxi business in 2017, but still kept on their insurance business and Cygnus meters.

John Paton went to Antarctica hunting whales to earn enough money to buy into the cab trade, which he did in 1957, in Glasgow. With his wife Agnes, he went on to build a very successful business dominating the Glasgow trade. Having gained the franchise to sell new vehicles Patons became the main dealer in Scotland. The business branched out into insurance, finance, taxi meters and body shop repairs. Being born in Govan, he was a lifelong Rangers supporter, joining the board in 1984 and becoming chairman, a position he resigned in 1986. He joined the board of Kilmarnock F.C. as vice chairman in 1989, a position he held until his death in 2001, having been predeceased by Agnes, in 2000.The business was then taken over by son Billy, whose son William and daughter Jill continue it today.As they have withdrawn from the taxi trade, the business now operates as Patons Accident Repair Centre.

When going to Patons in Glasgow for a service, it was amusing to see taxis lined up waiting for them to open, only to have Fred Newman walk down the line and tell certain drivers to go away as they had not paid their bill. It was also a brave man who would challenge Agnes Paton, she was a formidable lady, but very fair.

A major problem occurred in 1986 when it was found that the leg of the chassis on some taxis was cracking and the only place recognized to weld it was Paddy McGowans on Niddrie Mains Road. Patons decided to sell an alternative vehicle the Fiat Scudo but it was not a success with only one being bought. Its successor the TW300 was met with the same level of apathy and it was not viable for dealers to spend the money required to allow it to pass stringent test of approval, so it quickly faded from the scene.

Fiat Scudo TW 200

When the licensing department decided to abandon the 25ft. turning circle, this gave rise to alternative vehicles being available to drivers. These were not purpose built, but rather van conversions. Many drivers, disillusioned with the current offering from L.T.I. opted for them, with varying degrees of success.

The first Mercedes M8 was passed in December 2007. Alec Sands was the owner. Gary Masterson put the first short wheel base automatic M8 on in August 2009.

In August 2008, a variant of the Vito was approved by the Public Carriage Office for use as a licensed London 'black cab'. The Vito taxicab includes electric sliding doors, electric steps and seating for six people. The Vito's rear-wheel steering enabled it to meet the P.C.O.'s strict Conditions of Fitness requirements, including a 25ft (7.6m) turning circle and wheelchair accessibility. The vehicle, a variation of the 'Traveliner' model, is built by Penso in Coventry.

The new taxi does not perform the famous U-turn in the same way as the TX and Metro models, but instead, it incorporates an electrically operated rear wheel system activated by a button adjacent to the steering wheel. This turns the rear wheels in the opposite direction to the front wheels, thus allowing the taxi to perform the same tight turning circle as the TX and Metro models. This system is only possible when the vehicle is travelling at less than 5mph, and if the vehicle goes over this speed while the LSM is active, it is deactivated, and the wheels straighten up.

Over the years the Mercedes Vito has proved very popular.

As was reported at the time, Edinburgh City Council were left red faced after a blunder by the licensing department.

After prolonged lobbying by Glasgow based Allied Vehicles, Edinburgh City Council changed their licensing conditions for taxis on June 1st. to allow the Peugeot E7 to be used as a taxi in the city.

It has however transpired that the council managed to get the width of the new taxi wrong by 6cm, so it does not comply with their new rules. The Council decided to maintain their original width restriction of 1.78 meters and the E7 vehicle does not comply with this.

Much to the Council and its leader Donald Anderson's embarrassment, they have had to recall a number of newly licensed E7 taxis from operation. The so called new "tin can taxi service" as it has been referred to in the Edinburgh press, has been put on hold until the Council can change the rules once again to suit Allied Vehicles. The meeting was scheduled to take place this Wednesday 12th. July 2008. This has led to calls from a number of prominent Councillors to stop changing the rules to suit individual commercial interests.

Councillor Philip J Attridge, Convenor of the licensing board and past chairman of the taxi licensing board said, "I'm told by Council employees that this mistake has been caused by a misprint. It is likely the Council Board dealing with this will apply for a variation in the new regulations but as far as I am concerned the whole matter should be referred back to the full Council. I am not in support of the

Peugeot E7 being used in Edinburgh. We used to have the youngest and best taxis in the country, but not any more. When the alternative vehicles come into use, our taxi ranks will look like a builder's convention. Why on earth did the Council agree to allow these vehicles when we have always had a perfectly good taxi?" He added "To make matters worse, it seems as though we are promoting a Peugeot product at a time when they are pulling out of manufacturing in the UK."

The error was even more embarrassing as the Council had spent two years looking at the issue and £20,000 of Edinburgh tax payers money.

The Council paid a leading transport advisory company to look into the taxi rules only to cherry pick from its recommendations and to allow Allied Vehicles to get its E7 converted taxis licensed.

Their decision in June 2008 has now prompted other manufacturers of converted taxi vehicles for an even larger width restriction to accommodate Mercedes and VW vans. This has prompted fears that the quality and uniformity of the taxi fleet in Edinburgh will diminish beyond the point of no return.

Currently it is a difficult time for Allied vehicles as the Transport and General Workers Union have launched a £1 million campaign asking the public not to buy Peugeot vehicles until the company agrees to keep their UK based factory.

The Council also chose to ignore two independent surveys. One from the taxi trade and the other, taking the views of the people of Edinburgh. Both these surveys showed that the vast majority of drivers and passengers wanted to retain the traditional Edinburgh taxi.

The Councils error left the trade in confusion. Drivers can't buy the E7 for use as a taxi as it is still not licensed. If the Council don't change their new conditions, the E7 will remain only fit for use as a private hire vehicle.

In June 2006 the Peugeot E7, the first alternative vehicle to the TX and the Metrocab was licensed. Eric Shade was the driver. These vehicles quickly earned the sobriquet 'fish vans' by traditionalists in the trade. In October 2007 the new improved E7 was introduced and Tam Noble was the first owner.

Cab Direct opened for business in New Lairdship Yards then moved to Turnhouse Road before shutting down in Edinburgh. They transferred business to Glasgow temporarily, while new, more suitable premises were sought. No after sales service was on offer, it will be sales only.

Part of the Allied Vehicles Group, Cab Direct already selling the E7 introduced the Tourneo based Ford Procab.

Many drivers nationwide opted for the vehicle based purely on price as it was cheaper than other alternatives. This was a decision many would regret with some believing that they had been sold a product that had inherent faults. They believed the dealer was aware of them but they were never mentioned during sales talk.

To say that drivers were less than enthralled with it would be an understatement. Dealers had to deal with drivers' complaints while sympathizing with them. Their hands were tied as it was Ford who were not making them aware that the vehicle should be run at 5000 revs for a period to clear the filters.

The consensus of opinion seemed to be that it was not fit for purpose as reported in the "Scotsman" on 17th June 2019.New taxis bought to cut harmful emissions in Scottish cities will have to sit with their engines running for more than an hour a day to solve a fault, drivers have claimed. They said the diesel particulate filters on models purchased to comply with impending tougher emissions controls, rapidly become clogged up with harmful pollutants such as particulates. The solution is to leave the engine on for up to 40 minutes twice a day to clear the filter – or costly and time-consuming oil changes which drivers said were setting them back £300 a time. £150 for oil change, the rest loss of earnings.

The problem affects the more popular of the two black cabs with the latest Euro 6 engines, the Tourneo-based Ford ProCab.

Only taxis with Euro 6 engines will be permitted in Edinburgh city centre from 2022 and Glasgow city centre a year later.

Edinburgh taxi driver Danny Tebb said his ProCab has had to have four oil changes since December 2020, and required an oil change every 2000 miles for the first year.

Colleague Richard Dourley has had nine in 18 months.

Tebb said: "I'm livid. The Euro 6's are clearly unfit for taxi driving. We have worked out each driver would need to do this twice a day. That's 40 minutes a day sitting stationary with the engine running to clean the filter." David Facenna, sales director of Glasgow-based Cab Direct, which produces the ProCab, admitted the Euro 6 standards had 'stretched manufacturers.' He said "There appears to be knock-on effects for vehicle maintenance, including more frequent oil changes." Ford has produced a prototype software update that allows a driver to manually initiate the filter clean. (as an alternative to oil changes) Ford said it was "Willing to hear from drivers with major issues." It said: "Short stop-start drive cycles generate more particulates, which is well within the filter's ability to handle and avoid clogging via a regeneration cycle when the engine's up to temperature, running for 20 minutes and under load."

With the new software upgrade the problem seemed to be cured with drivers reporting no need for oil change in over 28,000 miles.

It is a fact that the cab trade over the years have supplied in many instances a first-class service using a second class vehicle. As long as the engine ran, the driver would put up with defects, many of which could have been easily rectified. But dealers seemed reluctant to tell manufacturers that in many instances their product was substandard.

WINCHESTER

The Winchester Taxi was launched in 1963 from Winchester Automobiles (West End) Ltd., a subsidiary of the Westminster Insurance Group. It was unique in that it had a glass fibre body and has the distinction of being the first to be built using this material. The Mark I had a Perkins diesel engine, the Mark II had a Ford Transit petrol engine, the Mark III had an all new chassis with a Ford petrol engine.

This taxi was not popular with the cab trade as they found it noisy, under powered and uncomfortable to drive. Passengers also had difficulty in using it as it had an integral step in the passenger compartment which they had difficulty in seeing, occasionally causing them to fall. It soon earned the nickname "The pick 'em up and pull 'em out cab." It is not surprising it never reached the sales figures required to make it a competitor to the Austin FX3 and FX4. The Mark IV launched in 1968 had a new shape body with a choice of either a Ford Cortina petrol engine or a Perkins diesel. The modifications made it a much better cab to drive but it was too little too late and the model ceased manufacture in 1972.

Stuart Hiddleston being presented with keys for the silver jubilee cab in 1977 from councillor from Licensing committee, with Ronnie Young looking on.

In the 70's and early 80's, owners wishing to upgrade their cabs would wait until a character known as "The Irishman" came to town. One day I picked up a fare who said, "Back of the rank in the Waverley Station driver." Strange destination I thought so asked him why. He told me he was here to buy up to 20 cabs. Pulling in at the back of the rank, which in these days was on the north ramp, he asked me to put a message over the air saying, "The Irishman is in the Waverley station and would later be at City Cabs garage looking for cabs." He had a Gladstone bag full of cash and as he got out, his jacket opened and I saw a gun in a shoulder holster. Asking him about it, he said he had a licence as it was for his protection because he carried a great deal of cash.

I asked him how much he would give me for my cab which was an S plate. "Too new for me." he said, "I only want old cabs." The story was that he came over from Belfast and bought cabs for the IRA and the UDA who then rented them out to drivers. They had already set fire to the buses, so the only transport was black cabs, each working their own area. Owners here who decided to sell were paid cash on the spot and told to take their cabs to the ferry at Stranraer in a weeks' time, load them, leave the keys in the ignition and his men would collect them over in Ireland. This gave the owner a chance to go to Ronnie Young and buy a new cab at a reduced price as they had no trade in. On the appointed day all the cabs would meet up and go in a convoy in case one broke down. An extra cab went with them to bring five drivers back.

Now the owners who had sold their cab were plagued by other owners to buy anything decent on their cab, seats, wheels, batteries bumpers even gear boxes were swapped.

The Irishman paid the drivers to deliver their cabs and even paid for the fuel, although it must be said that the cabs were breathing fumes by the time they were loaded on the ferry and how they got some cabs started again remains a mystery.

Chapter 11

Cab Inspectors

In 1819 an application from a Peter Wilkie to be appointed Superintendent of Hackney coaches was refused.

Robert McInnes received an annual gratuity between 1824 - 1829 and in 1842 Inspector McInnes had a salary increase.

Thomas McInnes was appointed assistant to his father in 1842 as inspector of Hackney coaches and in 1849 the appointment of Robert McInnes was recalled and Thomas was appointed with an increased salary and a petition from Robert McInnes to have his salary continued was not entertained. Robert McInnes died in 1851, bringing to an end quarter of a century of family dominance. On the recommendation of the magistrates, George Cooper was appointed but did not take the post up immediately as council minutes show that a payment was made to William Connel as interim inspector. Mr. Cooper was the Hackney Carriage inspector in 1866.

The Hackney Carriage Department was formed in 1855 and at that time was a Corporation Department with officials appointed by the Magistrates.

The first motor taxi cab was introduced on the Capital's streets on 6th. July 1907 and these vehicles operated alongside the horse drawn variety for some time.

With the introduction of mechanical vehicles, it brought additional problems to the department and with more and more motorized vehicles and less and less of the horse drawn variety, it was becoming obvious that they would need to be controlled by the police. However, it would only take 26 years for this to be put into practice.

At a meeting of Sub-Committee, A of the Lord Provosts Committee on 23rd. January 1929, a letter was submitted from the Clerk to the Magistrates with reference to the salary of the Hackney Carriage Inspector and his Assistant. This letter stated that the present Hackney Carriage Inspector was appointed to that post in June 1917 and his present inclusive salary was £390 per annum, the last increase to his salary being given in 1924. No maximum salary has been fixed for the post.

The Magistrates are of the opinion that the appropriate maximum salary be £450 per annum, and they recommend that the salary be increased to this amount by two annual increments of £30. They also recommended that in the case of any new entrant to the office the commencing salary be £350, rising by annual increments to £450.

In the case of the Assistant Hackney Carriage Inspector, the present Assistant Inspector entered the service on 16th. October 1919 and his present inclusive salary was £270 per annum.

The Magistrates were of the opinion that the appropriate maximum salary would be £330 per annum and they recommend that his salary be increased to this amount by annual increments of £10. As regards any new entrant, they recommend that the commencing salary be £250 rising to a maximum of £330 per annum by annual increments of £10.

The Sub-Committee, after consideration, resolved to recommend that approval be given to these recommendations so far as regards the present holders of the post of Hackney Carriage Inspector and Assistant Hackney Carriage Inspector, and that no action be taken as to the scales of salaries for future holders of these offices.

On the retiral of Peter Blackhall on the 22nd. July 1933, the Hackney Carriage Department was transferred to the Police, with a Police Inspector in overall charge with his salary paid for by the Council, which remains the case today. The duties of the department remained the same with the exception of the work involved in connection with 'property lost and found' in Hackney Carriages which was transferred to the police 'Lost Property Office.' During the same period the following proposals were accepted by the Magistrates,

1) to abolish the fare and a half night tariff for Hackney Carriages.

2) To require all taxi-meter gear boxes to be fitted with pegs in such a manner that they could not be rotated by hand.

In his first annual report the Cab Inspector stated that the following licenses were issued
  Motor Hackney Carriage 278
  Horse Drawn Hackney Carriage 10
  Motor Hackney Drivers 378
  Horse Drawn Carriage Drivers 14
  In 1978 there were 485 licenses issued

The Cab Office was situated in the Cowgate at the foot of Fishmarket Close until the early 1970's when it moved to the newly built police Headquarters at Fettes Avenue. Due to the cramped conditions, it then moved to the Police Garage on Henderson Row in 1979.This was the original cable winding station for cable cars and the winding wheels can still be seen on the east facing wall.

On 14th May 1990, the new Taxi Examination Centre on Murrayburn Road was opened by Lord Provost, Eleanor McLaughlin.

In what remains a mystery, it was extensively damaged in an arson attack and many historical documents were lost. An intensive police enquiry took place but no one as yet has been charged.

In 2009, the setting and marking of topographical examinations was taken over by the Councils Licensing Department, leaving them with only vehicle examinations and enforcement of licensing conditions.

Cab Inspectors.

Brown (1943)
Hollywell (1946)
S Kinnear (1948)
R. Brownlee
I McLaren (1954)
R. Welsh (1962)
J Dickson (1962)
W Scott
T Hogg
G Fairbairn
G. Till
J Bullen
J. Currie
R. Rutherford
(known as Rantin' Rab)

Alec Russell
Hugh Findlay (1986-)
Alec Elgin
Jim MacKenzie (1994)
Tom Purdie
David Wilson
Gordon Hunter (2000)
Murdo McIvor (2000-2002)
Andy Watt (2002- 2007)
Audrey Fry (first female 2007-2009)
Frank Smith (2009-2017)
Keith Mailer (2017)
A Smith
A Struthers

Fares and Licenses

In October 1947 there were 350 taxis licensed.
The cost of a cab drivers license in 1958 was 5/- shillings (25p)

1968	415 licenses
1979	515 licenses
1982	540 licenses
1986	627 licenses
1988	630 licenses
1988	812 licenses
1989	992 licenses
1990	1023 licenses
2010	1263 licenses
2017	1320 licenses

The 1980's saw a much-needed change in the way the cab office operated, when certain established practices were challenged. One of these was the driving test taken by successful applicants of the topographical test. This consisted of taking one of the staff for a drive, usually to the bakers or post office in Stockbridge. The practice ceased after it was challenged as the member of staff had no qualifications to be a driving examiner.

In other cases, it was found that it was the cab inspectors interpretation of the Licensing Conditions and would not stand up to a legal challenge. A breath of fresh air blew through the building when John Blain was appointed as an examiner. John served his time as a mechanic with Moir & Baxter in Comely Bank who were agents for the FX3.

John was a very fair but strict examiner who treated the cab owner with a bit of respect, but beware if you tried to pull a fast one. John would go on to be the senior vehicle examiner until his retirement. During his time as the senior examiner a disturbing incident occurred. One Wednesday night in the mid 1990's, a petrol bomb was thrown through the window landing on John's desk. Fortunately, it happened at night and no one was hurt, but a lot of archive material was lost. His private car was also targeted outside his house. The inspector at the time was Tom Purdie, a descendant of Tom Purdie, the first captain of Hearts football club. After the attack Tom took early retirement and went on to become head of security at Tynecastle Park. He is the author of 3 books, "Hearts: The Golden Years" and "Hearts at War." Tom also authored a book "The Scottish Junior Cup."

The appointment of Alec Russell as cab inspector was another step forward. Between him and John Blain, they changed the perception of the cab office by the cab trade putting an end to what was seen as petty infringements.

When Alec Russell retired, he took up a position as head of security at Easter Road Stadium.

Not all of the changes were welcomed by the cab trade as what had been a simple exercise now turned into a bureaucratic nightmare. In 2014 the Council took over running the cab office from Police Scotland, which inevitably led to changes in the system. When renewing your license, instead of going to the cab office, paying your fee and walking out with a new license, the procedure now takes on average two months and all too frequently, much longer. Many in the cab trade see the situation as another example of the Councils disregard for the trade.

During the time when the cab office organized the topographical test, the applicant was told that day if they were successful or not. They could ask to see their test paper to find out where they had gone wrong. Now that it is held in the City Chambers, the applicant can wait up to a month before finding out their result and they are not allowed to see their paper, so in the event of a fail, they do not know what they failed on.

One of the most popular cab inspectors was Andy Watt. After thirty years in the police, mainly in Roads Policing, he was appointed Cab Inspector. Inspector Watt held this position for five years, from 2002 until his retirement in 2007.During this time he participated in several fund raising events. The taxi trade gave a great deal of support towards these events which included climbing mountains in Africa and Vietnam, cycling across Israel and taking children to Lapland to see Santa Claus. The charity was CLIC Sargent which gave support to the families of children with cancer and leukaemia. Andy and his wife also fostered children with special needs, and they continue in retirement to do so. A few years after retiring, Andy was diagnosed with cancer which was successfully treated, and he is now enjoying good health.

The AUSTIN
FX4 TAXICAB

Much improved

after 6 years' operational experience

FX4 PRICES (Ex Works)

DIESEL (Synchromesh) £1,245
DIESEL (Automatic) £1,325
PETROL (Synchromesh) £1,170

SECOND-HAND TAXICABS
AVAILABLE
FX3/FX4

Enquirers please state
type and price range required

Sole Retailers for Metropolitan London:

MANN AND **OVERTON** Ltd
—————ESTABLISHED 1899—————

298 WANDSWORTH BRIDGE ROAD, S.W.6

Telephone: RENown 4484 (4 lines)

Join The Edinburgh Team
The Goal of Every Owner

THE NEW
AUSTIN TAXICAB

Always on top of form

Great on the Hills

Light on the Bills

Place Your ORDER NOW with the Distributors

MOIR & BAXTER, Ltd.

COMELY BANK GARAGE, EDINBURGH

Telephone 30134-5-6.

Throughout the whole Taxi Trade
Interest is focused on...

THE 2·2 LITRE
AUSTIN
DIESEL F.X.3.D. TAXICAB

**PRICE—
£1,041 10s.**

(F.X.3 Petrol Engine Taxicab-£936 10s.)

Sole London Concessionaires

MANN & OVERTON LTD
298 Wandsworth Bridge Road, S.W.6

Telephone RENown 4484 (4 lines)

1957 taxi advert

Chapter 12

Cab Trade Legends

Kenny Cuthbert's taxi repair company on Lower Gilmore Place was a step back in time. It was dark, dirty and it had not changed since Kenny opened up. He had his regulars who would swear that he was a genius. Specializing in the repair of Metrocabs, there was nothing he did not know about them. Referring to everybody, no matter their age, as "son" he soon became a legend in the cab trade. He was prone to be slow in sending out bills which maybe accounted for some of his popularity, indeed some owners never received their bills at all and to their eternal shame, never questioned it. However, on the ranks they would sing his praises about how he was a great guy but obviously not good enough to be paid.

Davie Clark relates a story about when he worked for Kenny. One day, Bryan Ford came to Davie asking for a chrome hub cap. He said, "Get me one and I will give you a fiver, but don't tell Kenny." Davie thought, happy days, so he put the cab on the ramp and took one off the opposite side, cleaned it and gave it to Brian and got the cash. As Brian was leaving Davie said to him, "Do you ken you've one missing on the other side as well?" At this point Brian went mental. The whole place was in uproar. Great times.

Bob McKirdy

Returning from war service with the R.A.F. in 1946, Bob gained employment as a mechanic with the Niddrie Mill garage. After ten years, he rose to become manager on a wage of £10 a week, but he decided to change direction after talking to cabbies whose cabs he maintained. He purchased a second hand 1954 Beardmore for £150. He remembers his first job, Princes Street at the Scott monument to the George Hotel and he was tempted to tell the fare that he could see the hotel but refrained. On disengaging, the fare gave him £4, nearly two days wages. He picked up a fare from the same hotel to the airport and he said, "I learnt a valuable lesson that day, it does not matter where the job is going, you never know what will follow." It was to be his philosophy until he retired aged 70. He was asked to leave City Cabs in 1967 for being involved in a scheme at Belford Road garage, namely repairing member's cabs and getting paid for it. He, along with his good friend, Gus Tyler, were thrown out at the same time. They both immediately joined Radio Cabs where they remained until retirement. A keen footballer, he played for Murrayfield Amateurs and Harewood United before becoming a cabbie. He started playing for E.C.A.T.R.A. and played in the annual match against M.O.C.A.T.R.A., a team of London cabbies. These games were played on a home and away format, depending where the Home International against England was being played. When the match was at Wembley, the Edinburgh cabbies would travel down to London and their game would be played at one of the top grounds, either Queens Park Rangers ground at Loftus Road or Fulhams ground at Craven Cottage. When the International was played at Hampden, the match would take place at Easter Road. After the game both teams would go and watch the International. These games developed into a social event with a dance being held which large numbers of cabbies attended.

In Bob's first game against the Londoners, he scored the winning goal in a 1-0 game. This feat would be repeated in his last game. In all, he played against the Londoners 15 times. He continued to play for E.C.A.T.R.A. before hanging up his boots, aged 62. At one of the matches in the 1950's, Bob and London cabbie Stevie Knight, suggested that they bring their golf clubs and so another annual event was started. This ran until the 1990's, when it was decided to hold the four day event at a neutral venue near Birmingham. The Mocatra club folded but Ecatra is still going strong. Bob continued to play golf at Gullane where he was a member for over 50 years. Aged 91, he invited me for a game, apologizing that we would need to hire a buggy as he could not walk the eighteen holes. For many years Bob was the secretary of E.C.A.T.R.A. golf section and he ruled it with a fist of iron, making certain that all members wear a collar and tie when visiting courses and adhere strictly to the R. & A. rules and the rules of etiquette. It was at the Marr Trophy outing to Haddington that he disqualified his son-in-law Billie Laing, who thinking he had won, forgot to sign his scorecard. When driving his cab Bob would always be seen wearing a collar and tie, and a blazer with the R.A.F. badge. On the dashboard he attached a vase which contained fresh flowers, although he admitted to me that he got them from the crematorium. Bob has the dubious distinction of being the first cabbie to be fined by the Inland Revenue for failing to keep accurate books. In the early days, the Inland

Revenue could request that the cabbie sign a mandate allowing them access to details held by the cab office, such as vehicle mileage and drivers' names. They worked to a formula to account for dead mileage and the mileage was then used to calculate, on a probable basis, how much the cabbie had earned. This practice was later successfully challenged as the mileage was unsubstantiated and the owner never saw what mileage was being recorded against his vehicle and it did not take into consideration odometers running fast.

Captain Bob McKirdy receiving the trophy after winning "International" against Mocatra at Easter Road stadium when he scored the winning goal.

Joe Costello

By anyone's standards Joe would have been considered a "scruff," always wearing bib and brace overalls. He lived with his wife in a flat on Haddington Place where his wife conducted seances.

He was involved in pony trotting (harness racing at Stenhouse stadium) with his stables in Thirlestane Road Lane. If any cabbie asked him for manure for the garden he would deliver in in the taxi. He would just shovel it into the passenger compartment. When asked by the cabbie how he would get it clean, his reply was "Ach, just gie it a hose out, it will be fine." Long time cabbie Ronnie Grant relates the tale of being stopped at traffic lights when Joe pulled up alongside him. Looking over, Ronnie was astounded to see 2 Shetland ponies in the back of the cab with their heads out the window. Joe's answer "I'm just taking them to the field for grazing."

The Provost

Finishing work one hot summers day, I called into the Hillburn Roadhouse for a cooling drink. While I was sitting at the bar perusing the paper, I was disturbed by a squeaky, whining voice enquiring if that was my taxi outside. On confirmation, the owner of the voice told me that he had been a cabbie before retiring. "Just ask any of the old timers. They all knew me, I was famous." A nutter I thought, as he got into a pointless argument with the bar staff. Finishing my drink and as I took my leave, he called out "Mind and ask about "The Provost."

A few days later I was talking to Jimmy Robertson, (known as "The Throm) Vice chairman of City Cabs and asked him about 'The Provost.' His reply astounded me. "That Bastard! He could start a row in an empty house. He was always starting arguments in the taxi canteen in the Caledonian Station. He even robbed the Murchies dairy on Lochrin Place but got a 'Not proven' in court."

He went on to explain that 'the Provost' who got his nickname because of his upper-class accent signed up for the first 'self-build housing' in the city on Redford Road.

He was contracted to work a certain amount of hours a week as well as paying his share of materials so every penny he had was accounted for. One night while having a meal in the Metropole cafe on Thornybauk, the police came in and arrested him. All he said was "It wisnae me." His cab was taken to the police garage on Henderson Row (later to become the cab office in 1979) for forensic tests. In the run up to the trial he kept repeating the same line. On the day of the trial, the High Street was jammed with abandoned taxis as the drivers fought to get a seat with a view of the proceedings. The case was that the office of the dairy company had been robbed by sledge hammer wielding thieves, setting off the alarm. Failing in their attempt to break open the safe, the thieves carried the safe outside and loaded it into the luggage compartment of a taxi. Within an hour, the taxi was found outside the cafe less than a mile from the scene of the crime. The empty safe was found the following day, in-between the dairy and the cafe. Screws from the safe were found in the luggage compartment, as were feathers of a type on the hens in the dairy. An eye witness saw the whole thing, jotted down the registration number of the taxi and called the police. The Prosecution opened with a strong Forensic case explaining that paint samples found in the taxi matched the paint on the safe and the screws found were identical to the ones on the safe. The eye witness told how he was just settling down to sleep when he heard the alarm. Looking out his window, he saw two men load the safe into the taxi before getting on board and driving off. He had a pen and paper handy and wrote down the number. On cross examination he admitted to having excellent eyesight and only wore glasses to read. As his bedroom was about 40 yards from the dairy and on the second floor, he could not see the driver and admitted that on the registration plate the letter S might have been a 5 and the letter E might have been an F and that the B might have been an 8.

When 'the Provost' entered the witness box, he told the Judge that the whole thing was a mystery to him and no matter how hard he thought about it, he could not understand how anyone could think he was involved. His explanation for the screws was that taxis were always in garages and the screws may have come from there. He said the police found them there, but he was not present at the time to confirm this and while not accusing the police of planting evidence, admitted that he could not explain the find. He also explained that he parked the taxi and went in for his meal and an hour later the police came in and arrested him. He said that there were no door locks on taxis, and anyone could get in at any time. (He did not explain that an ignition key was required). When the jury returned a 'not proven' verdict, the judge was stunned, as were the police. The cabbies in the public gallery gave a rousing cheer. When I met him again a few days later I quizzed him about the case, all he said with a sly smile and a wink "It wisnae me." He completed the house build and lived there until his death.

Mention of City Cabs garage on East London Street and one name stands out, Bob Crawford (V132). The stories about him were the stuff of legends. One evening just after 9pm., going home to Gilmerton for his supper, he was hailed by a man who had had a few drinks and was standing at a bus stop on Clerk Street. Thinking he was going south, Bob pulled up. The man got in and said "Danderhall." Bob thought, 'Ya beauty! That almost takes me home.' The man promptly fell asleep. Driving up the road Bob started to think about what he would see on telly and drove straight home, parked the taxi and went indoors. After he had his supper, he came back to the taxi around 10.30 and getting in, noticed that the meter was still running. While trying to figure out how this could be, he heard snoring from the back of the cab. Remembering where the man was going, he started the cab, restarted the meter and drove to Danderhall. Approaching Danderhall, he shouted to the man to wake him up and asked where he should drop him off, as the usual place was the hole in the wall on the Old Dalkeith Road, and so it turned out. When the man was paying, he asked Bob what time it was, and Bob told him it was a quarter to eleven. "How the f*ck is that? I left the pub at 9 o'clock" the man stated. "Their clock must be slow" Bob told him and dropped off a very confused man.

Bob was a stalwart of the howf, always ready to lend a hand to anyone whose car broke down on the night shift. He never charged for any work no matter how long the job took, all he asked for was a cup of coffee from the machine, price 20p. Many a driver got a weekends work after Bob repaired their cab, myself included. He would tackle any job, no matter how big.

But Bobs enthusiasm was not always matched by his knowledge.

On one occasion V22 came into the howf and complained that his watch had stopped, and he could not get it started again. Bob said he would take a look at it and proceeded to take the back off the watch. The assembled drivers watched in fascination as Bob proceeded to take the watch apart without the need of a jewellers loupe (apparently you don't need one) and placed the parts on his thigh. After a few minutes he started to reassemble the watch and told Blabs (V22), whose watch it was, that it was fixed. The assembled drivers looked on in amazement as Blabs put the watch on his wrist. "It's working!" he announced. Then someone noticed a part of the watch was still on Bob's thigh. "What's that?" he was asked. Without missing a beat he said "You don't need that bit. I had one in my watch and I took it out, a damn pest they are" and proceeded to throw the part in the waste paper bin. After a few minutes Blabs looked at his watch and it had stopped. Removing it from his wrist he got up and walked out the door and without saying a word dropped the watch in the waste bin. This caused a great deal of hilarity and Bob was never allowed to forget it. Some years later, Bob tragically died and at his funeral all his pals from the night shift were gathered around the grave. Giving the eulogy, the minister mentioned how Bob would always help his fellow cabbies and he could turn his hand to any repair, including watches. At this point the cabbies looked at the ground and dared not make eye contact with each other. Alan Moir, seeing Skoogs shoulders shaking, and thinking he was overcome with grief, put his arms round his shoulders to comfort him before realizing that we were all laughing quietly, remembering the incident in the howf.

After the funeral, the night shift adjourned to the Stable Bar and as it was a sunny day, sat outside in the courtyard where stories about Bob started to be told amid gales of laughter. The barman brought out a tray of drinks and hearing the laughter, asked what the celebration was for. Blabs looked at him and dead pan replied, "We just buried our mate, he was a good guy." This caused more laughter and the barman retreated with a confused look on his face. As his brother Andy remarked "At the grave side, I could not look at any of you bastards as I would have burst into laughter." A fitting tribute to one of the trades good guys.

One of the garages frequented by drivers was Pettigrews on Jordan Lane. When Hugh Pettigrew died, the business was run by his wife, known to the trade as Mrs. Antiquary, due to her liking of the amber nectar. The head mechanic and later owner was Charlie Spence, one of the most knowledgeable but bad tempered men you could meet. His stock answer to you when trying to describe a fault was "You just fu**ing drive it, leave the brain work to me." If you were slow in paying your bill, he refused to work on your cab. His reasoning was, you got paid when the job was done, so he was entitled to the same privilege, but if you paid on time, he would work all night to get you back on the road. One day while working on a cab and lying on a crawling board fixing an exhaust, someone came into the garage and shouted "Hello." This was ignored by Charlie and again someone shouted "Hello." Again Charlie ignored it. This time, the man thinking he had not been heard, tapped Charlie's ankle with his shoe... big mistake! Charlie flew from underneath the cab and leapt to his feet and eyeball to eyeball, brandishing a hammer demanded, "Who the f*ck do you think you are kicking?"The man, completely taken aback, explained that he was taking his car next door to Gerry Martins for an MOT and thought he would take the opportunity to call in and introduce himself and compliment him on the high standard of cabs he produced for their annual inspection.The man was Jimmy Burns, vehicle examiner at the cab office.Charlie's response "Well you've done that.Now f*ck off and let me get on with my work."He was a hard man to work with, firing both his brothers.He was better working on his own as he felt he could do the job better than anybody, which was probably true. He solved faults in cabs that had defied Patons mechanics for ages.

"Big Deek"

Derek Brown or "Big Deek" as he was known to all the cab trade was a stalwart of the childrens outing for many years. He won best dressed driver as Worzel Gummidge in 1980 and in 1998 transformed his cab into the Starship Enterprise from the TV show Star Trek winning the best dressed taxi competition. Due to his enthusiasm he was invited onto the organising committee.

As a committee man there was no harder worker, from selling immune badges, raffle books and emptying taxi banks in licensed premises nothing was too much bother for him.

He was made "Transport Manager" responsible for the hiring of vans needed on the day and it is to his credit that he managed to get them for nothing telling the companies that the free advertising was worth it. As he was unmarried and rented a room in a house he led a lonely kind of existence his only interest was the outing. One of his jobs on the day of the outing was to entertain the Glasgow cabbies who came through for the day. He was invited to go on the Glasgow outing and this started a tradition that would continue for many years. Through his involvement in the Glasgow outing he received the freedom of the City of

Glasgow. It was typical of "Deek" that he never told anyone, not even his brother who only found out when sorting out his affairs after his death.

When he became chairman in the early 1990's he was critical of any committee member who was not pulling their weight. This led to confrontation with the secretary who decided that "Deek" and the treasurer should be fired. A meeting with the trade was called. The trade backed them and they were allowed to continue in their posts. However the situation was becoming impossible and the treasurer resigned leaving "Deek" as the only committee man querying how the outing was run.

A double blow suffered in 2002 changed the course of his life. First the secretary convinced the committee that "Deek" should be fired and at the same time he failed the medical to retain his licence to drive a taxi due to the worsening condition of muscular dystrophy a disease he had battled for years. These decisions, taking away the only two loves in his life had a devastating effect on him. He lost the will to live and his brother arranged for him to be taken into sheltered accommodation in Wrexham where he contributed to his own death in 2008

The Coroner who described his habit of self harm as the cause of death said that "Deek" had a "Calvinistic work ethic and could not cope with a sentence of effectively a living death". He added "This was a man who had given up" and gave a verdict of death by misadventure.

"Deek's" criticisms of the secretary were vindicated in 2005 when the secretary was replaced and in an act of vengeance he reported the outing to the Environmental Health department of East Lothian council in an attempt to get the outing cancelled. This strategy backfired spectacularly when the health officials visited the site of the outing and declared the food preparation area it to be of a very high standard with only one minor fault and gave high praise to Rab Veitch and his team of volunteers.

Alan McStay (P55)
(The Wee Fat Man)

A long standing member of Central Radio Taxis, Alan with his sense of humour, put into verse the day to day experiences of cabbies, always managing to make the most frustrating experiences seem funny.

His poems covered many topics relating to cab driving and were published in Central Taxis newsletter.

Sadly, Alan died in February 1985 and his poems were sadly missed.

A Cabbie

You're up in the morning early
And you're working late at night.
It doesn't matter what you do
It seems you're never right.
"Yer takin' me the long road"
Or "an awfy driver you"
Or "mind how you lift my cabin trunk
I've packed nice and fu'"
The moans are never ending
But you've got to take it all,
Or there's the Cab Inspector,
Aye, he's always at their call.
Still, you get a lot of nice folks,
and they help to make your day.
They smile and they say, "Thank You."
No matter what they pay.
These are the folks like you and me
who never treat you shabby,
and make you feel there's a lot worse things
Than being a bloody cabbie.

Public Relations.
June 1981
The taxi driver is much abused
in lands both far and near,
but there is something you can do
to stop the rot right here.
For courtesy and civility
is not too high a price
no matter what they are like to you,
to them you must be nice.
Treat them as valued customers,
not as your sworn foe
and always think about yourself as a taxi PRO.
We know when taxis hit the news,
the picture's always bad,
they don't publicise our good points
which we really think is sad.
But there is a way to beat them,
with their comments on our trade,
to get the public on our side is a valued aid.
We pick up folks of every class,
every colour, creed and nation,
From pubs, hotels and houses,
from airports, bus stops, stations.
They look to us, the first they meet
as typical of the Scot
so it's up to us to let them know
we are a friendly lot.
To let them see that this is not
a land of drunken louts,
despite the tales the English FA
try to spread about.
Oor ain folk too, do not forget
provide our bread and butter
so give them service with a smile,
don't leave them in the gutter.
Be patient with the elderly,
Or the man that's slightly fu'

You never know, one of these days
it might be me or you.
So do the best lads to provide
a service that is great,
and you will win the punters back again
Before it is too late.

Two of the most memorable characters in the taxi trade were Alan D Hogg and Bob Smith.

Both were a bit non-conformist to the perceived way a taxi driver should act according to various taxi companies committees.

Bob Smith

Bob Smith who always wore a tartan suit became known to the public as "The Tartan Cabbie" and to the trade as "The Tartan Terror". Picking up a fare in his white taxi complete with disco lights, he would enquire what their taste in music was and then play some tunes from his vast collection of tapes.

The stories about him are part of the cab trade folklore. One day he picked up an American couple and took them on a city tour. They said they would like to sample some traditional Scottish food for their evening meal and asked Bob what he would recommend and would he join them. Bob duly obliged, he purchased three fish suppers and drove them to the castle esplanade where they could enjoy the sunset while listening to a tape of the pipes and drums of the Royal Scots Dragoon Guards.

The Americans were very much impressed and declared it the highlight of their visit and that their diver was "Just Awesome".

He was a great stalwart of the childrens outing winning best dressed driver and proudly displaying the winners trophy in his cab. He would also dress up as Santa Claus at

Christmas and the Easter Bunny at Easter giving Easter eggs to any children he had as passengers.

Seeking permission to wear a kilt, this was refused by the cab inspector failing to take into account this is our national dress and that many lady drivers wore skirts.

Dispatched one night to pick up the cab inspector from the ex-servicemen's club on Steads Place and take him home to Colinton Mains, he stopped at a fish and chip shop on Comiston Road and told his fare he would be back in a minute. Returning with a fish supper an infuriated cab inspector (known as Rantin Rab) enquired what the hell he was playing at. Not at all fazed by his passengers demeanour Bobs response, "By the time I drop you off the chippy will have closed".

Alan D Hogg

"Alan D Hogg, advanced driver" was how he liked to introduce himself.

Joining the taxi trade after working as a postman in the Royal Mail South West delivery office he caused management plenty of headaches and they were no doubt overjoyed when he left.

Prior to a visit from one of the senior management team to inspect the efficiency of the depot all the staff were told to be on their best behaviour. On the day of the visit everything was going to plan all the postmen were at their stations sorting mail, a no smoking order was in place and all coffee cups were out of sight.

Just as the visiting dignitaries were leaving the managers office to inspect the sorting office one of the postmen knowing Alan's talent for mimicking cartoon characters, asked in a loud voice if anyone had seen T.V. last night as there had been a cartoon of "Foghorn Leghorn" Alan rose to the bait and leaving his sorting position started to walk up and down between the sorting frames flapping his elbows and shouting at the top of his voice in a very accurate rendition of Foghorn Leghorn "Ah Say You Boy. Ah Say You boy" much to the delight of the postmen, shock and anger from the manager and complete disbelief from the visiting brass. It would not be long before Alan hung up his uniform and became a cabbie.

He very quickly fell foul of taxi company committees and soon had various chairmen scratching their heads in disbelief at his antics. But the average cabbie saw someone they could have a bit of fun with. One summers night over the radio came the warning "Take care Corstorphine Road. Black Ice" the regular drivers knew this was the code for a police check point and speed trap.

However Alan was unaware of this and told control he would indeed take care. The rest of the fleet realising he did not know what the message really meant, decided to have a bit of fun. Calling into control they asked what conditions were like in Clermiston. Alan being a bit naive said he would give it a look, after five minutes he called Control and gave the all clear. What about Broomhouse? enquired the fleet, again Alan said he would give it a look. After getting the all clear the fleet enquired what about Wester Hailes?, again Alan said he would check it out. This continued for another hour before Vic MacLean the controller lost patience and shouted at the fleet to leave him alone so he could earn some money. All the time Alan was unaware of what was happening and at no time did he stop to think that there was no chance of roads freezing over in June.

Chapter 13

Independent Taxi Services

There are quite a few adjectives, none of them complimentary, that the cab trade could use to describe Mark Greenhalgh and Jimmy Neilson.

Mark Greenhalgh (ex V31) a man of short stature but big ideas, was better known to the trade as 'The Penguin,' not for his liking of dark suits but more for the fishy smell permeating from his ideas. It was in the 'howf' at City Cabs garage on East London Street that Penguin first met Jimmy Neilson (ex V42) and where the regulars first got a glimpse of how he alone had the answer to all the ills affecting the trade. Part of his strategy was denigrating City Cabs committee at numerous A.G.M.'s in an attempt to gain enough votes for him to be elected to the committee. He finally succeeded in 1997, but his success was short lived as his behaviour whilst on the committee upset many of the membership, which resulted in an Extraordinary General Meeting being called in 1998 with the sole purpose of the membership deciding whether or not he was a good representative of the company. The membership voted overwhelmingly to remove him from office.

Jimmy Neilson, or to give him his paid for title, Neilson of Sclattie, served for many years on City Cabs committee but his biggest claim to fame was in being the prime mover in having the owners name removed from the taxi door, claiming it would be beneficial on security grounds.

Both Greenhalgh and Nielson got together with other cabbies and formed the Edinburgh Hackney Cab Trade Credit Union in 1995, one of the best things they were involved in. When the Credit Union first started, Greenhalgh was Chairman, Neilson was Treasurer and the registered office was 8 Argyle Place, Neilson's personal residence. Jimmy's son Keith was appointed secretary. Unfortunately, many cabbies would not join as Greenhalgh was involved, and the Credit Union suffered as it did not grow as big as it should have done.

Using their position on the board of the Credit Union, they secured a place at the Taxi Liaison Group meeting of the Council where they pushed through their ideas that prospective members of the trade would have to sit 6 modules in addition to the topographical test. It was their stated aim to have a 'One stop organization' where every aspect of the cab trade, from liveries to knowledge schools, modules to plate transfers, would be centred with Greenhalgh as a self-styled taxi supremo.

Starting up a company called Independent Taxi Services in 1996, they started selling advertising space on taxis and putting up £400,000, they started Cabtivate in May 2003. They had LCD screens fitted into thirty taxis in Edinburgh for a trial period of six months to iron out any hardware problems before being rolled out nationwide and then worldwide

It was a wonderful business plan except for one small fact, large numbers of the Edinburgh Taxi Trade did not trust them, so their market in Edinburgh was always going to be limited to a small number of owners who would be taken in by the projected figures produced by Cabtivate. As Greenhalgh told me, "They come into the office potless with their arse hanging out their trousers looking for any sort of handout. They will believe anything if they think they will make a few quid".

Greenhalgh would have been well advised to heed the statement of American President Abraham Lincoln, "You can fool most of the people some of the time and you can fool some of the people most of the time but you can't fool all of the people all of the time." His prediction was that the company would have a turnover of £1.2 million with screens in 710 cabs in its first year. In year two, a return of £3.8 million and in year three, £7.8 million with screens fitted in over 2,000 cabs. In reality, this was never more than pie in the sky from someone whose thinking was at best deluded. His attempt to have the screens fitted in every new purpose built cab supplied by John Paton & Son came to nothing. When owners refused to buy a vehicle if it had a screen fitted, his total disregard for the views of the cab trade and his 'nanny knows best' style of thinking was another example of how out of touch he was with his potential customers. The aim was to have 25% of licensed cabs in Edinburgh and Glasgow signed up, meaning 350 cabs in Edinburgh and 380 in Glasgow.

In an attempt to gain financial backing for Cabtivate, Greenhalgh went on the television programme Dragons Den and offered the Dragons 10% of the company for £100,000. But he stuttered, stumbled, forgot his lines and got his figures wrong. The four entrepreneurs panned him and the product, telling him it was outdated technology and would never work. Duncan Bannatyne summed up his performance with the quip, "Well that was cabtivating." The next morning DVD's of his humiliation were on sale at East London Street with proceeds going to the kids outing fund. The clip can still be viewed on you tube.

In an attempt to save face and convince cabbies that all was well, he was soon bragging in the press that the Dragons had got it wrong and that he had investors lining up to give him money. He said he had secured very big contracts, one of which was the Strathclyde Police. He managed to convince over 200 cabbies in Edinburgh, Glasgow, Manchester, Liverpool and Bristol that it was good business to give him £4000 for an LCD screen. Greenhalgh promised to pay the drivers £192 a month, giving them a profit of £88 a month. Alarm bells started ringing when finance director Iain Mackenzie resigned on December 4th 2006, with cabbies complaining that they had not received money due to them.

In early January 2007, Cabtivate were still signing up drivers to the system, but on January 22nd. Greenhalgh and Neilson petitioned for liquidation with debts of almost one million pounds. This included a £100,000 investment from Scottish Enterprise. Accounts for the company show that in its last financial year, it had an asset deficiency of £375,000 after seeing losses more than double from £466,000 to £957,000. Amounts owing to creditors rose from £312,000 to £483,000 during the year. The intellectual property rights to the company were bought by Russian media company iMTV who rebranded the company as Cabtivate Networks Limited and received testimonials from Murray Fleming of Central Radio Taxis and George Aird of City Cabs. On January 25th.2007, a new company Tapinto, with a registered office in Milton Keynes was registered with Companies House.

The director was Mark Greenhalgh. The new company would supply LCD screens to private hire vehicles. The initial idea was to fit the system into 50 cars working the airport.

In a statement on September 14th. 2007, regarding the takeover by iMTV Greenhalgh said, with typical arrogance, "I can't tell you how glad I am about that. I now feel vindicated, particularly after months of unjustified attacks on my character from the small number of people left out of pocket by the collapse."

In January 2010, ITS and the Edinburgh Hackney Cab Trade Credit Union, which Jimmy Neilson was treasurer, closed down amid allegations of financial impropriety and for failing to supply accounts to the Financial Services Authority for two years. Despite repeated requests and by doing so, was failing to satisfy the FSA that it was conducting its business soundly and prudently and in compliance with proper standards.

Unfortunately, there were a number of people who would lose thousands of pounds.

At the time of its demise, the credit union had 203 members. Ten of whom were directors, who must take a share of the blame, as they did not keep a tight enough grip on proceedings which allowed the situation to get out of control.

The number of members were only a tiny proportion of the people eligible to join, perhaps reflecting the opinion in which the trade in general held them.

Chapter 14

Taxi Regs

The subject of wheelchair accessible taxis was first raised at a licensing sub-committee meeting in May 1987. A report from the Cab inspector in June 1987 showed that only two licensed taxis were wheelchair accessible. Owners Iain Scott and Bobby Williamson had their cabs modified to take wheelchairs, paying for the modifications themselves with a promise from the Secretary of State that they would receive a grant, which never materialized. The sub-committee resolved that the City Council should formally investigate ways in which the number of wheelchair accessible taxis in the City could be increased.

In May 1989, the then City of Edinburgh District Council, used the Civic Government (Scotland) Act 1982, to set a requirement that all new taxis licensed should be wheelchair accessible. It set a target date of January 1997 when all cabs licensed in the City would be wheelchair accessible. At that time, operators working from the airport, persuaded the council that they should be exempt from the regulations because their passengers needed saloon car comfort for long distance journeys. However, in October 1995, the City of Edinburgh Council resolved that all airport taxis should be of the purpose-built variety (Metrocab, FX4, TX1) and be wheelchair accessible by 31st December 1999.

In the interim period, they also specified that all airport taxis be fitted with swivelling front seats to improve access for mobility impaired passengers.

In November 1997, the Council amended its policy by the removal of the specific requirement that the vehicle be of the purpose-built type agreeing to continue consultation regarding suitable wheelchair accessible vehicles.

The view of the council officers was that it would be cost neutral to the council to have all vehicles licensed wheelchair accessible, as the increased cost of a wheelchair accessible taxi would be borne by the operator.

The Council run Handicabs dial-a-ride scheme was in financial difficulties and needing a cash injection of Council money. Getting taxis to do this work would save the council money. It was a classic win - win situation for the Council.

The unit cost of subsidized taxi trips under the taxi card concession scheme is less than the cost of providing such journeys on the dedicated Handicabs dial-a-ride service. This saving would not be possible if taxis were not wheelchair accessible.

One of the better ideas started in 1976 was the introduction of a knowledge school run by Duncan Peden under the auspices of the Edinburgh Taxi Owners Association. (ETOA) However, the way it was run and with different owners taking different classes on a weekly basis there was no continuity and after a few years the project folded. There was no structured way of learning how to pass the taxi exam until Jimmy Kerlin started the Kerlin Taxi School. Over the forthcoming years, he would help hundreds of men and women to pass the topographical test until 2019, when he retired due to ill health. But he did not have it all his own way. Bob Dewar, (known to the trade as neurotic Bob) started the Taxi Academy until he also retired through ill health.

The District Council decided in 1972 that country work beyond the eight-mile limit was to be charged at fare plus one half, i.e. £30 = £45.

In an attempt to preserve work to areas outside the licensed area but inside the eight mile limit a series of surcharges was introduced by radio companies.

The practise of starting the meter when given a radio job which led to confusion to customers as the amount on the meter when the cab arrived varied. This depended on where the taxi was when dispatched. To avoid this a hiring charge of 40p was introduced.

1983 saw Central Radio Taxis drop the 40p hiring charge in an attempt to win customers. City Cabs decided to do the same with contract customers, only Radio Cabs decided to retain it.

A tragedy occurred in 1987, when a child fell from a moving taxi and was killed. The child had been sitting on a tip-up seat and attempting to open the window, opened the door by mistake. Esther Rantzen started a campaign on television for door locks to be made compulsory on new vehicles. Existing cabs were fitted with a plastic guard over the internal door handle.

Chapter 15
Ecatra Football

The cab trade had many sporting clubs all coming under the banner Ecatra.

Ecatra was formed in 1924, but records show that their predecessors were also very much football minded. Representative matches were played between Edinburgh Cab Drivers and Edinburgh Taxi Drivers in the years 1911 and 1912.Going back even further, an annual competition was inaugurated in 1896 between cab drivers from the east and west areas of the city. A Mr. Somerville presented the trophy (which became known as the Somerville Cup) and the last game in this series was held in 1912.

When the club was formed in 1924, their first bid for honours was in the Mid-Week Amateur League. Five years later in season 1929-30 they finished top of the league. Shortly after this, they transferred to the Tuesday Amateur league for convenience.

Football activities were suspended during the war years, but in 1947, Eddie Smeaton, club secretary, was instrumental in getting the league restarted and it went on to comprise sixteen teams in two divisions. Winning many trophies, Ecatra with their fast style of play, became the team no one relished playing. In winning the league in 1952, they lost only one game, when they were beaten 5-3 by Telex. Playing in sky blue tops, their home ground was Leith Links, where they were virtually unbeatable. As a child I watched them when they played St. Margaret's or Beechwood at Pinkhill. The attraction being their goalkeeper Gus Wardrope, who wore a ginger wig. Before the kick-off, Gus would throw the wig into the back of the net for good luck, much to the amusement of the watching children and he quickly became our hero.

The team of the early 1970's could boast three sets of brothers. John (Soapy) Sutherland, known as cannonball because of his ferocious shooting ability and his half brother John Crawford, the brothers John and George (Dode) Anderson and Willie and Brian Smith, brothers to the legendary Gordon Smith of Hibs and Scotland fame.

Paddy Crossan, a Heart of Midlothian player, fought as one of McCrae's Battalion during the First World War. On retiring from the professional game, he became a publican on Rose Street and suggested a match between Edinburgh and Glasgow taxi drivers. It was Paddy who donated the medals for the first match in 1928.

In the autumn of 1928, following two friendly games between the taxi drivers of Edinburgh and Glasgow, the editor of the "Taxi World" put forward the suggestion that an "International" football match be arranged between a picked team of Scottish taxi drivers and a similar team from among that fine body of sportsmen who comprise the London cab trade. As was anticipated, the suggestion aroused the utmost enthusiasm both North and South of the Tweed. When the British Taximeter Company kindly offered to put up a Challenge Cup and the Beardmore Taximeter Company, with equal kindness, agreed to present two sets of specially designed medals, plans were speedily prepared for the holding of the first "International" sporting event in the history of the British Taxicab industry.

Kick-off at Manchester City's Ground in the first game of the series in 1929. Photo shows Alderman CHRISTIE starting the game. Referee is SAM COWAN, Manchester City's "International" goalkeeper and beside him the respective Captains.

Kick off inaugural "International" Maine Road 1929

The following is an extract from the Manchester Evening News.

Manchester was chosen as the venue for the encounter, the Directors of Manchester City F.C. having kindly offered the free use of their magnificent ground, and the Manchester and Salford Owners and Drivers' Association expressing pleasure at the opportunity of giving their fellow drivers from London and Edinburgh a generous sample of Lancashire hospitality. The Chief Constable of the City (Mr. J Maxwell) and Alderman Carter; Chairman of the Hackney Carriage Committee, along with other members of the City Council evinced the keenest interest in this sporting enterprise of the cab trade. Alderman Carter agreed to perform the kick off ceremony while the Chief Constable (a Scot by the way!) not only attended the match, but also the celebration dinner in the evening, whereat, in presenting the cup and the medals, he paid glowing tribute to the fine sporting spirit of taxi-drivers as a whole.

The Scottish Taxi Trade's representatives returned to Edinburgh on the morning of Thursday, April 18th 1929 with the cup, having defeated the London *Mocatra* team 1-0.

The proceeds of this match were given to the widow of a Manchester taxi driver, who had been killed in an accident when he drove into the Manchester Ship Canal during a thick fog. Since then the proceeds of the annual match have been given to a charity and many hundreds of pounds have been raised over the years.

In the following year, 1930, the match between the two cities took place in Edinburgh; on Wednesday April 9th on the famous Tynecastle Park ground, kindly placed at our disposal by the Directors of 'Heart of Midlothian F.C.' Once again civic recognition was accorded the cab trade. Bailie Dickson, one of the senior Magistrates of the Scottish capital and Chairman of the Hackney Carriage Committee, kindly offering to kick off and afterwards to present the cup and medals to the contesting teams.

His tribute to the inherent sportsmanship of taxicab drivers was no less eloquent than that of the Chief Constable of Manchester, while the cab trade of Edinburgh gave their colleagues from London abundant proof that a Scot is second-to-none when it comes to dispensing hospitality.

As to football skill, there was little to choose between the English side and the Scots, but the latter retained possession of the cup by a 2-1 victory over the *"Mocatra"* eleven. The medals that year were presented by Messrs. W. Watson & Co. (Liverpool) Ltd., the distributors of the Morris-Commercial taxicab.

Mocatra Athletic Club founded in 1922 is the acronym for the Motor Cab Trade an organisation in London promoting sport in the cab trade with sections for angling, cricket, rifle shooting, darts, golf and football.

Some of the attractions at these games were the officials; in 1949 the linesmen were Tommy Walker (Hearts) and Eddie Turnbull. (Hibs)The game being played at Easter Road and Scotland winning 1-0. In 1950 the linesmen were

Tommy Walker (Hearts) Gordon Smith (Hibs) at Easter Road with Scotland winning 3-0.

1952, again at Easter Road, the linesmen Willie Bauld (Hearts) and Willie Ormond (Hibs) Scotland won 2-1.

The 25th Meeting between the clubs took place again at Easter Road Stadium in 1954 and the linesmen on the day were Willie Bauld (Hearts) and Willie Woodburn. (Rangers)The Scots would be 3-2 winners taking their total wins to 11 with England 6.

In 1956 at Easter Road, the linesmen on the day were Bobby Parker (Hearts) and Willie Ormond (Hibs) with England 2-1 winners.

In 1965, the game was played in London, with Bobby Robson (Fulham and England) the referee. Scotland won 2-1

In 1965, George Dent secretary of Mocatra, donated a trophy for 'Man of the Match.' This was won by H. Gordon. (Scotland) The first double winner for Scotland was John Wilkes (V62 &166) 1975-76 and 1982-83 and John Graves (V71) won in1978-79. The winner in 1983-84 was Andy Coventry (Scotland) with an outstanding display in goal.

It must be said that the cabbies have a better record than their professional counterparts against the Auld Enemy, winning 54 times to their 23.

'International' winners medal, runners up 1948 and Edinburgh v Glasgow winners medal 1928.

Mario Crochini presents Alan Moir with the Tait Trophy after a 4-2 win over S.M.T. Claymore. Two weeks later they would go on to win the league after a successful visit to London where they beat their English counterparts.

Winning team 1971

| G Irvine | J Gunn | W Moncur | D Strickland | R Hunter | A Moir | J Ramage |
| T O'Neill | J Graves | J Sutherland | J Robertson | J Rudkin | | |

LONDON WELCOMES THE SCOTTISH TEAM

Eddie Smeaton senior, lays a wreath to remember fallen taxi drivers at the Cenotaph in 1953, during a visit to play in "International" football match.

In 1983 Ecatra played Mocatra in Scotland's football kit from the 1982 World Cup in Spain. No one will admit as to how they acquired them. Were they nicked from the team coach? By co-incidence, team manager John Graves was in Spain for the World Cup.

Back row Alan Moir, Alan "zoom" Robertson, Alec Kemp, Frank Walls, Stuart McCabe, Dougie Lamb, Aly Bain
Front row Aly Blythe, John King, Paul Connelly, George Smart, Gillie Sebastion

| Top—Taxi-Drivers F.C. 1 9—24 Bottom—Taxi-Drivers F.C. 1 9—49 |

J. Ross A. Duff. R. Paton. A. Hedderick. L. Gaudie. G. Watson. W. R. Young
W. Milne. G. Binnie. G. Hume. A. Watt, Cpt. J. Doctor. H. Alexander.
W. Hunter.   E. Smeaton.

F. Archer   H. Alexander.   J. Guthrie.   W. Young.   J. Laidlaw. E. Smeaton, Sy.
D. Reid, W. Moffat. W. Robertson. A. Wardrope. J. Anderson. Cpt. D. Baillie. P. Thomson
R. Macintosh. S. Livingstone. S. Gilhooley. J. Groat. R. Clarkson.

Chapter 16

Ecatra Golf

Ecatra Golf was formed in 1949 by a group of Edinburgh cabbies including Wilson Cooper, Wullie Flockart and J. Shepherd. (the good shepherd) They played their golf at courses around the city and Tuesday became known in the trade as Golf Day. The club was run on very strict rules,

1) That every member must be a working cabbie.
2) That jackets, collar and ties must be worn when visiting clubs.
3) No loud behaviour that would reflect badly on the name of the club.
4) Strict adherence to the rules of etiquette and the rules of golf.

These were rigidly enforced with a "bad book" where members names were recorded with any complaints against them. Too many complaints and the member was expelled. A.G.M.'s were held at Ratho Park Golf Club until 1982. The first trophy that they played for was donated by Archie Marr, a publican. This trophy is regarded as the big prize with every member desperate to add his name to the illustrious list of past winners. The trophy is played for each August at a venue which is kept secret until the day before to stop the pot hunters having a secret practice. The only people who know the location are the Secretary and the Treasurer. A bus is provided to the venue, where after two rounds a winner is found and everyone can relax in good company at the social night and perform their party piece. There have been a number of good performers over the years, but Chic Robinson with his rendition of 'The Wee Cooper O' Fife' doesn't fall into that category. Tam Doyle, who on opening a fridge door and the light coming on, could do twenty minutes of a stand-up routine with his endless poems that emptied the hall. Stalwarts of the club over the years have included Alec Wren, Jack Chrystal, Bob McKirdy, George Mather, the Alexander Brothers, Willie and Jimmy, Billie Laing and Peter Haggart.

At the reception following the annual football match between Mocatra and Ecatra, it was suggested that a golf match be arranged between the two clubs. This was duly arranged and started in the early 1950's and would run for 45 years until Mocatra golf club folded due to financial reasons in the late 1990's.

Hugh Pettigrew was the first captain to lead the team to an away victory and win the Cresswell trophy in London in 1963. He sadly died in 1969 while President.

As with any club, the golfing stories are usually very funny or cruel, depending on your outlook. When Dougie Logan fluffed a pitch and in a fit of temper threw his club away, unfortunately it stuck up in a tree. A part time fireman returned to the course at night with a fire tender to fetch it back down.

Dennis Rogers, known as the "Flashing Blade" who after taking thirteen strokes to get out of a green side bunker and whilst raking the sand did not see Ian Sneddon kicking his ball back in. Bob Marjoriebanks, who whilst playing Mortonhall in the final pairing and needing a 5 to win or a 6 to tie at the par four eighteenth, hit his drive to the middle of the fairway. It landed in the perfect position to approach the flag. With the whole club watching on the clubhouse verandah, he took 12.

Aly Gardiner (ex V176) was the team captain in 1988 when Ecatra almost completed a white wash of the Londoners. The only ones to lose were the red hot favourite pairing of Billy Laing and Peter Haggart.

Aly remembers; I was privileged to be involved in many of these four day matches during the 1980's and '90's. Sleep was a dirty word, but many memorable days and nights were spent with our brothers from the 'Big Smoke.' On many occasions I witnessed big tough cabbies from the east end of London leaving the Waverley Station with a tear in their eye, after four days of mayhem around Edinburgh.

Ecatra A team Gullane 1988

Ecatra won all three trophies losing only one match
Back row Peter Haggart, Colin Davidson, Gordon McCausland, Ian Rendell, Donald Fleming, aka Sneaky Pete.
Front Row Bill Mitchell Ali Gardiner (captain) Jas Ward

Mocatra A team Gullane 1988

Chapter 17

Edinburgh Taxi Trade Outing for Crippled Children

Annual Outing
By Alan McStay
April 1980

Children laughing, clapping, shouting,
It's the Taxis Annual Outing.
Happy kids, forgetting pain,
feeling normal once again.
Wheelchairs, crutches, plaster casts,
Taxis dressed as ships with masts.
Moonships, spaceships, made by dreamers,
covered in balloons and streamers.

At Murrayfield the big parade,
important choices to be made.
The best dressed taxi, they must choose,
though one must win, the rest must lose.
But every driver gets his prize,
from the look in little children's eyes.
And every driver plays his part,
to get into each child's heart.
The helpers and the nurses too,
are all entitled to their due,
for giving up their time and leisure,
to help bring all the children pleasure.
Lifting, feeding, wiping, sharing,
soothing, comforting and caring.
All for love and no mean ration,
of understanding and compassion.
Happy children now are tired,

the day has passed, now sleep's required.
An end is called to all the fun,
the homeward trek has now begun.
Balloons deflated, drivers too,
streamers limp, like the helping crew.
Memories made without a tear
and plans start now for another year.

A Special Fare.
May 1981
The time once more has come around,
when taxi drivers must be found
to do their bit and volunteer,
as they do each and every year,
for the sake of the kids who need a break
bringing happiness in their wake.

These mites, who've had a deal so rotten,
have to be shown they are not forgotten,
disabled in body or mind
with happiness so hard to find.
We'll try to wipe away each tear,
more so in this, this special year.

So rally round lads to the cause
be like a summer Santa Claus,
and give the kids what they are after
joy and happiness, fun and laughter;
so they will forget their aches and pains
in taxis dressed as ships and trains.
Balloons and streamers all the way
to give these tots the finest day

Jim Kerlin winning balloon cab

Bob McCulloch winning float

Known affectionately to the cab trade as the "Crippled Kids" but due to political correctness it has had to change names more than once.

Since it started, thousands of children have had a day out to remember, thanks to the generosity of the Edinburgh Cab Trade. What could be better than driving through the city en-route for Yellowcraigs (nowadays Archerfield) in a highly decorated cab with a water pistol at the ready to soak any unsuspecting policeman or traffic warden?

First started in 1948 by the welfare committee of Edinburgh Licensed Hackney Carriage Association, with 20 cabs taking 40 children on a day out to the beach at Gullane, before relocating to Yellowcraigs in the 1970's. It grew to 100 cabs taking 250 children and helpers.

Eddie Smeaton, Hon. President, who never missed an outing for 40 years, and who latterly drove the pick-up truck, was full of stories from the early outings which his father had helped to start. After World War II and with food rationing still in force, it was difficult to get potatoes, but someone heard of some stored in a farmers barn. So it had a visit from some night shift cabbies and the children got their mince and tatties.

When the cabs met at Murrayfield Ice Rink, they were judged in two categories, best dressed cab and best balloon cab. There is also a competition for the best dressed driver and best dressed child. The winner of the best dressed taxi receives the Willie Merrilees Trophy, donated to the outing by Willie Merrilees, OBE Chief Constable of the Borders Police force. Willie, a staunch supporter of the outing, came along each year to act as a judge and to lead the convoy to Yellowcraigs.

The outing traditionally set off from Drummond Place but on the grounds of safety, it moved to the car park at Murrayfield Ice Rink in 1978.After judging, the convoy moves off at 10am. As the cabs make their way through the city, many workers stop work and come out of offices and shops to join pedestrians and tourists to give the children a wave. Children from primary schools along the route are lined up waving flags (and getting soaked from water pistols in return) but their turn will come in the afternoon when on the return journey, they lie in wait with water pistols, garden hoses, and anything that is capable of projecting water, much to the delight of the kids in the cabs.

Before it closed, when passing the Lothian & Borders Fire Rescue Service Training School in Gullane, the trainee firemen would be lined up to give a wave and as usual the kids would reply with water pistols, but unknown to them at the end of the line there would be a fire engine with its hoses turned on which caused panic in the cabs to get the windows closed.

A comfort break is taken at Musselburgh where Luca supplies free ice creams, as they have done for over 70 years.

Next it was a lunch stop at Aberlady Community hall where everyone enjoyed mince and tatties followed by either ice cream or trifle.

A sing song accompanied by Alec Bartleman on the organ and compered by Micheal Borys proved very popular before heading to the beach.

Due to required repairs on the community hall, the committee decided to have a barbecue on the beach. This proved to be popular. Its popularity has continued thanks to Rab Veitch and his team of helpers. One of these was Jessie Clark, a relation of one of the original organizers and it was she who became the sort of organizer of the helpers. After many years she dropped out leaving Margaret Whitson, Irene McGubben and Rita Graham to carry on. They retired after their 40th Outing when the committee made a presentation to them.

The stunts the drivers have pulled over the years to entertain the children are almost beyond belief. Ray Forrest, who had served in the Household Cavalry, hired horses and with friends dressed as red Indians armed with tomahawks, bows and arrows and whooping war cries ambushed the convoy and chased it to Musselburgh.

In June 1977, George Dougall was awarded the British Empire Medal for his work on the committee of the Handicapped Children's Outing, but sadly died before he could go to Buckingham Palace to receive the award. Ian Clark then took over as secretary.

Eileen McCallum presents keys to Neil Gushart watched by Denis Durnam and committee members Eric Fortune, Derek Brown (Big Deek) Chairman, Bob McCulloch treasurer.

To celebrate the 50th anniversary, the committee decided to do something special. Several special needs schools whose pupils came on the outing suggested a facility where families could have a holiday. A large fund-raising operation was started with the aim of purchasing a caravan, specially adapted to take wheelchair users. The cost of purchasing and adapting the caravan to accommodate wheelchair users was £15,000. This was achieved, and the caravan was situated at Thurston Manor caravan park near Dunbar. At the opening ceremony, performed by Eileen McCallum, the actress best known for her role as Isabel

Blair in the S.T.V. series 'Take the High Road' presented the keys to Neil Gusthart of Tranent. Many families and representatives from the Social Work Department attended and were suitably impressed with the facilities. A buffet lunch and cabaret were supplied by the site owner Dennis Durnam.

Belarus children 2009

2009 saw a welcome new addition to the outing with the presence of a group of children from Belarus who were suffering from the after effects of the fallout from the Chernobyl nuclear power plant in the Ukraine, which exploded on 26th April 1986. The explosion released clouds of radiation which drifted over a wide area. The children were in Scotland for a break and a health check-up, thanks to the 'Friends of Chernobyl.' They were invited on the outing and a mini bus was hired. It was explained to the organizers the format, detailing the need to provide water pistols. On arrival at Murrayfield, they looked a bit out of place with small hand held pistols when all the other kids had supersoakers. On the journey down to Yellowcraigs they had great fun squirting people until they ran out of water.

It had been explained to John Galloway that due to contamination they could not drink milk back home and they needed to drink it here. This set John on a mission. Contacting a dairy and explaining the situation, dozens of cases of flavoured milk were received. When they were about to leave Yellowcraig, John gave the organizers the cases of milk to take away. Now on the return journey all the kids en-route, line the streets with water pistols, garden hoses anything to project water at the cabs. The kids from Belarus, seeing what was happening and realizing they were out of ammunition started to fill their water pistols with milk. When I spoke to the organizer the next day, she told me that the children said it had been the best day of their life, and they were so excited they could not sleep. As for the organizers, it was not such a good day as they were up until 2am. washing out the mini bus to get rid of the smell of milk.

Due to changes in thinking within the social works department, there are not the same numbers of children who are now eligible, so the number of taxis now required is just over 60.

In the early 1980's, John Graves, winner of best dressed taxi with his taxi decorated as a log cabin, was invited to take part in the Edinburgh Evening News Festival cavalcade where he won best float. I had the privilege of winning two years later and was invited to lead the jazz parade along Princes Street at the start of the Jazz Festival. The highlight of the day was Will Gaines tap dancing the whole way along Princes Street, while keeping up a conversation with me through the luggage compartment window.

Over the years there have been many wonderful stories about the kids outing and of the many characters who have taken part. Stars from the world of television, music and sport have given their time to come along and meet the children and let them have their photo taken with their heroes. These include representatives of Scottish Rugby who displayed the Calcutta Cup, from football Hearts and Hibs with the Scottish Cup and Josh Taylor with his world super lightweight championship belt who was a great favourite with the children and drivers.

Special thanks must go to legendary fund raiser Tom Gilzean, who over the years raised hundreds of thousands of pounds for the outing and the Royal Hospital for Sick Children. Sadly, Tom died on 5th November 2019 aged ninety-nine.

One of the stalwarts of the outing was George Gardiner (known to the trade as Socks) who always made a special effort for the day and who won the competition for best dressed cab, best balloon cab and best dressed driver.

His cab dressed as a dinosaur, was covered in 5000 balloons and with a 20-foot neck, won best balloon cab. Everything went well until the procession was entering Prestonpans when the head of the dinosaur got caught in the overhead phone wires and pulled them down.

His escapades were many and varied but his commitment to the outing was second to none.

After winning best balloon car a couple of times he wanted to win best dressed taxi but did not know how to build a float, so he asked me to help. What followed was an eye opener.

First he scrounged all wood, cardboard, and printing ink, sourced a classroom in Q.M.C. but had to buy two felt tip pens for a total of £1.60, only because the shopkeeper was watching.

The theme was a cartoon cavalcade with all Disney characters, life size and hand made. He also arranged the use of a shed in Leith Docks to build the float and we set to work.

He got the Bank of Scotland to donate 20 rucksacks, which he filled with sweets and drinks, all donated by Bellevue Cash and Carry.

On the morning of the outing, I went to his house to help him get ready. He was going as an African woman, so we started covering him in black body paint but ran out and had to finish with black shoe polish. To complete his costume, he had a pair of plastic boobs sprayed black and a grass skirt. His pick up was Douglas House, part of the sick kids hospital. When we arrived, he told me to bring in the rucksacks and boxes of sweets. Going into the ward, he attempted to give the nurses a cuddle, but they wisely bolted, much to the amusement of the kids.

He then told the kids breakfast was cancelled and they would have to eat sweets instead. He then started a competition to see who could jump the highest on their bed and who could shout the loudest. The prize being more sweets. Within minutes the ward was in chaos. Standing at the door was an auxiliary who was supposed to give breakfasts but was now redundant. She said to me I must go and get the nurses. Thinking Socks had gone over the top, I suggested I would get him to calm down a bit but she said "No! Look at the boy over there. He has lain on his bed for two weeks, never moving or speaking, but now he is jumping on his bed eating a Mars bar. This is the start of his recovery." When the nurses saw this, they had tears in their eyes.

On leaving, each child not coming on the outing was given a rucksack full of sweets and told they had to eat them all before we came back or else.

That year Socks won best dressed taxi and best dressed driver. He was the first to do so. When being presented with the trophy, he embraced the cab inspector and some of the black body paint came off onto the inspector's white shirt, ruining it.

This was at the time the outing stopped at Aberlady, and many drivers went to the Wagon Inn for lunch. I went ahead to get a table and order food.

The only space available was at a table with two elderly American tourists. Sitting down and waiting for Socks, I got into a conversation with them. When Socks arrived, he caused mayhem with the waitresses and when he sat at the table, the American woman could not take her eyes off him. Sitting with her fork poised, halfway between plate and mouth, she gazed in wonderment at the vision before her. Socks noticing this, said to her "I love children." She replied, "I can see that." Then he returned with, "But I couldn't eat a whole one."

One completely baffled American. The couple insisted that they would pay for our lunch if they could have a photograph with George and his cab saying, "They will never believe this back home." Good Times.

Jimmy and George Muldoon (V23) were great supporters of the Kids Outing but tried not to let it interfere too much with the object of making money. On the Monday before the outing, the night shift would start around 6 o'clock and work until 2am, then go to R.B.S. garage on Robertson Avenue where other cabs were being decorated. This was a fun time with many families getting involved helping to decorate each other's cabs. By the time V23 arrived, most cabs were finished so everyone pitched in to help them. Everyone had to be out by 6am, so it was home for breakfast before picking up the kids. The Muldoon brothers took it in turn to go on the outing as it was the one on day shift, and that year it was Jimmy's turn. He met George at Robertson Ave and helped decorate the cab. Arriving at Murrayfield, Jimmy was dressed up as Frankenstein, which scared the kids (but not as much as the members when he became chairman of City Cabs.) A lovely warm sunny day was most welcome and arriving at Yellowcraigs everyone was having a great time. John Lumsden came running up to me and told me Jimmy Muldoon had collapsed. We hurried over to behind the tents and there we found Jimmy sprawled out on the grass. Giving him gentle prods with the foot and calling his name, we got no response. While waiting for the first aid team, a few drivers gathered round giving completely crazy suggestions. Then Skoogs stepped forward and said "I know how to revive him." Crouching down, he yelled in Jimmy's ear, "1st. call North Berwick." Immediately, Jimmy sat up and with eyes still closed, raised his hand to his mouth as though using a radio hand set and shouted, "V23, V23 back in the car in Dirleton"

Conclusion - never get between Jimmy and a £1 note.

Pete Tye was a London cabbie for many years. All his family were involved in the Tradex Insurance Company. Pete was a stalwart of the East London taxi outing and one of the original drivers on the Magical Taxi Tour to Euro Disney. Sharing a few beers with him in Disney, he related the story about the time when he was younger and a West Ham supporter. He, along with others, decided to come to Glasgow for the Scotland v England football match in the Home International series. This was the oldest international football match in the world having been started in 1874 and sadly cancelled in 1984. Arriving at Glasgow Central station on an overnight special train from London, the Londoners, not all completely sober, were a bit boisterous singing and chanting as they made their way to Hampden.

The Glasgow police, who are not known for their softly – softly approach, rounded the supporters up and herded them back onto the train bound for London. Before the train departed, they were warned that the next time they came to Scotland they would be arrested.

Pete expressed a desire to come on the Edinburgh kids outing and this was arranged for the following year. By this time he was semi-retired and living in Portugal, but he flew over for the trip. Ian Booth gave him a loan of his taxi, which had the Tradex livery and it was a very proud Pete who joined the convoy. Stopping in Musselburgh at Lucas for ice cream, we went upstairs for a coffee and a bacon roll. I told Keith Bell about his trip to Hampden and Keith arranged for the motor bike cops to arrest him. As Pete was leaving the cafe, a policeman asked him his name and could he prove it. Pete, going into his pocket, produced his passport and asked what the problem was. The policeman looking at his passport told him "You were warned what would happen if you came back" and produced a pair of handcuffs which he put on Pete and led him out of the building. The look of disbelief and confusion on Pete's face was priceless. After a good laugh, he phoned his daughter in London and said "The bastards only arrested me. I can't believe it." It was one of his best memories of the cab trade. Sadly, he died six months later.

Chapter 18

motto
With Knowledge We Serve Crest
Worshipful Company Hackney Carriage Drivers

To enable Cabbies who had successfully passed the Taxi Tour Guiding Course and to display a sticker depicting The Worshipful Company of Hackney Carriage Drivers coat of arms these needed to be matriculated by the Court of The Lord Lyon.

At a ceremony in July 2014 attended by the Master Graham Woodhouse and Officers of the Court along with members of the Edinburgh cab trade, cab inspector Frank Smith and councillor Eric Milligan were presented with the certificate by the Lord Lyon.

The company decided that the proper place for this to be kept was Edinburgh, so it was presented to the Lord Provost where it hangs in his office

Lord Lyon Dr. Joseph Morrow presenting certificate of Matriculation to Master Graham Woodhouse

Chapter 19

A Magical Trip with a Special Boy

In 2006 the organizer of the Children's' Magical Taxi Tour for children with life limiting illnesses asked me if my son Neil and I would pick up two families from Middlesbrough and take them on the outing.

Arriving at police H.Q. where we had arranged to meet the families, we met James Marshall and his parents. James aged 5, suffering from a brain tumour, was partially sighted and unable to walk a great distance so was in a wheel chair.

He had got his first pair of shoes for the trip as up until then, he required leg braces. We set off, heading for our hotel in the Docklands area of London where we would spend the night. In the morning we met the rest of the tour for the Big Breakfast which was attended by the Lord Mayor and the High Sheriffs of the City of London. During all this time, James never said a word.

His behaviour was repeated on the drive to Dover and on the ferry to Calais.

On the drive to Euro Disney and at the evening meal, James still had not spoken. There was virtually no response from him at all.

Next morning we were up bright and early and into the park with James in his wheelchair. I asked Rachael, his mum, if there was anything special James would like to see. She told me that he loved Peter Pan, so we headed for the Peter Pan's Ride Over London attraction. Taking James on the ride, we used our special pass to go to the front of the queue. Sitting next to James, I took his hand in case he got frightened. When we saw Peter Pan, I could feel his grip tighten and he started to laugh. When the ride ended, I asked him if he would like to do it again. As we came off after the second ride he shouted to his Mum "I saw Peter Pan" and he was very excited. This was the first time I heard him speak. His mum threw her arms round my neck and started to cry saying she had never seen him so excited before. Going around the park was great fun for him but we always had to go back to Peter Pan.

After our day in the park it was time for the Gala Dinner. After the meal, all the Disney characters came into the hall for a party. James was sitting in his wheelchair when Pluto came over and snuggled up to him. This was followed by Mickey, Minnie, Donald Duck and Goofy all coming over to shake hands with him. He was so excited, he got out of the wheelchair and joined in the dancing. Seeing this, Rachael was overcome with emotion and cried with happiness. Definitely a night to remember. On the way home, James was very animated when we played silly games on the ferry. This was not the same little boy we took away four days previously.

Arriving back at police H.Q. in Middlesbrough, James's granddad was there to meet us and was astounded in the change in him saying "I have never seen him like this before."

Before we said goodbye to them, Neil unscrewed the license plate from the rear of the taxi which had been made specially for the trip and gave it to James as a memento. When they returned home, Rachael fixed the taxi plate above James's bed to remind him of his time with us. She later told me that James was admitted into mainstream schooling shortly after the return from the holiday and that he was doing well.

Sadly, the story does not have a happy ending. The tumour grew and despite various treatments borne bravely by James, he died on 29th May 2012, eleven days short of his eleventh birthday. Rachael put the taxi license plate James had been given on his coffin. She went on to run marathons and raised enough money to sponsor a taxi 'In Memory of James Marshall' on the outing in 2013.

Rachael and her mother came down to Canary Wharf to wave the taxi convoy off. She wanted another child to experience the trip of a lifetime and asked if my son Neil would be the driver. It was a very emotional time for everyone.

The only comfort we can take from this is that we gave a little boy some happiness in his tragically short life. When people ask us why we do these outings, we tell them the story of James Marshall.

Chapter 20

Tales from the Rank

When Dire Straits were playing in the Playhouse and staying at the Carlton Hotel, they booked a cab to take them to the venue for a sound check. After dropping them off, the driver picked up another fare. When the lady got in she noticed that there was an attaché case on the floor, gave it to the driver and said "I hope it's not a bomb." I had better get rid of it then, thought the driver. As he was passing a building site where a rubbish skip was sited, he thought it to be the perfect place, and heaved the case into the skip. The pop group, having realized that they had left part of their equipment in the taxi, phoned the company to have it returned. The controller identified which driver had done the job and asked him where the case was. He explained he thought it was a bomb and had dumped it in a skip and was now miles away. The controller then asked the fleet, who was the car nearest to the street where the skip was positioned. The nearest car was Wee Jimmy Craig so he was dispatched to retrieve the case and return it to the theatre. When he arrived, he found a tramp searching among the contents of the skip with the case in his hand. Wee Jimmy, who was not known for his sartorial elegance, told the tramp to hand over the case, but was told where to go. Seeing that the derelict was not going to hand over the case, Wee Jimmy climbed into the skip to take it from him. While they were wrestling for possession, a police car pulled up to see what the commotion was, and soon had the combatants out of the skip. They refused to believe Jimmy was a taxi driver and it was only when he went to the taxi and spoke on the radio that the situation resolved. That was the day 'Skippy' entered the Cab Trade legend.

When I picked up a fare going to Penicuik, I decided that it would be my last job for the day. En route, we passed a group of soldiers wearing large rucksacks, running towards town. My fare, who was in the army, explained that they belonged to the Parachute Regiment and that they had been dropped off at the other side of Penicuik. They had to make their way back to Redford Barracks and that they had a certain amount of time to complete this exercise. As we passed, I noticed that in any group of runners, there are always the ultra fit who are well in front, followed by the majority who are reasonably fit, then at the rear, the ones who spend too much time in the NAFFI. Dropping my fare off at Glencourse Barracks, I headed back into town. It was not long before I came upon, in the last group, a lone soldier, struggling to keep going, sweating heavily and barely able to lift his feet. Pulling up alongside him, I asked if he wanted a lift as I was going home and lived near the Barracks. His reply was "Thank God. I think I'm going to die." He took off his rucksack and got into the cab. The first thing he did was light up a cigarette. Continuing into town we soon came across the other group and I asked him if we should stop and pick up some others He replied "F**k them! Leave them to run." Getting off his seat, he crouched down on the floor. " Don't want these bast**ds to see me," he explained. When we came across the leaders, he peeked up to see who was leading the pack. "No surprise there! It's the P.T. I. show off. Wanker!" was his comment. He went on to explain that the last eight men back to the Barracks would have to do guard duty the following weekend, while the rest got a weekend pass. He had recovered by the time we reached the Fairmilehead crossroads, saying "Just drop me here mate. That's great. I will manage from here." I should hope so, I thought. It's only about a mile and a half. Off he set, with a definite spring in his stride and I was left to wonder what the leaders would think when they got back to find he had beaten them. That was the end of the story I thought, until one night, a few weeks later, I got a job to pick up at the Ensign Ewart pub, going to Redford Barracks. Five squaddies got in, not drunk, but definitely in high spirits. One of them was the soldier I had given a lift to, but a little nod of the head was all the recognition I received. During the journey, over the radio came a message that one of the company driver's was being attacked by two thugs who were attempting to rob him. One of the soldiers asked me "Are you not going to help your mate?" I explained to him that I was engaged and the incident was quite a distance away. "F**k that! Let's go and help!" When we arrived at the scene, the elderly driver, Jimmy Hopper, was being attended to by another driver. Jimmy's face was covered in blood from a head wound caused by one of the thugs hitting him with an iron bar. Jimmy told us that the two men who attacked him had run off into fields which were part of an adjacent building site. The five soldiers took off into the darkness. After a short time we could hear a series of whistles. The police and ambulance arrived and Jimmy was taken to hospital. Taking statements, the police asked me what I was doing and I told them about the soldiers looking for the thugs. After a while, the soldiers returned with their clothes covered in mud, telling the police that they hadn't caught them. They got into the taxi and we set off for the Barracks amid much laughter and high fives. Arriving at the Barracks, I told them that there would be no charge and thanked them for their assistance, adding that it was a pity that the thugs had gotten away. Amid gales of laughter, I was told, "No they didnae! We caught them and they will be in hospital for longer than your mate. They will be okay. They should be found in the morning." Giving me a £20 note, they said that they had enjoyed their night out. I told them that they could be traced by the police and their answer made me laugh. "Who cares? We are off to the Falklands in the morning." It made me feel kind of sorry for the Argentinians.

The night shift controller, Jackie Robertson, told me that she was writing a story about the time she worked in the control room of the ambulance service. She received a call from a hysterical woman who could only scream "OOOOH, IT'S MY HUSBAND! IT'S MY HUSBAND! HELP! HELP!" Getting her to calm down, she informed the lady that the ambulance was on its way. When the crew returned, Jackie asked them what had happened. They told her that a night shift taxi driver had taken a bath and went into the living room, still naked, to dry himself in front of the fire. His wife who was hoovering down the side of the armchairs and feeling a bit playful, began to run the arm of the vacuum up and down his body. Unfortunately, he must have been feeling a bit fruity as well. His penis got caught in the suction pipe. He panicked - she panicked - and a very painful tug of war took place between them. If they had remained calm enough to think (if indeed anyone could in this situation), the wife could have switched off the cleaner, and disengaged, so to speak. But by the time they realized this it was too late and he was well and truly stuck. After a few minutes the husband was rational enough to think to phone for an ambulance. As he was still attached to the infernal machine, he found it difficult to manoeuvre the cumbersome companion to the phone. His wife therefore made the call but was still so incoherent that she could not explain what had happened. When the crew arrived, the ambulance driver, who thought he was a wit, suggested sending for an oxy-acetylene burner. This sent the wife off again, wasting more time. The ambulance driver calming them down, told them that in twenty years' time they would look back on this and have a good laugh. He then added wickedly "It may be in a soprano voice, but you will laugh." The crew could not remove the man from the machine so took him to hospital, causing a great deal of hilarity at the Accident and Emergency. Picture the scene, two ambulance men carrying a stretcher upon which lay this man with a huge lump in the middle of the covering blanket. The ribald comments of the doctors and nurses infuriated the man, but he was hardly in a position to give them a piece of his mind. He probably was hoping that they were not going to get a piece of anything at all from him. Relating the story in the garage to the night shift drivers, we were wondering who it could have been, when Tommy tight trousers exploded with "If she mentions my name, I will sue the Bitch."

Dropping off a fare at the city's newest four-star hotel, the passengers told the driver that they were attending the evening reception of a very smart society wedding. They had been anticipating the festivities for some time as this would be the first wedding to take place in the hotel. With the number of guests attending the sit down meal and the evening reception, it must have been costing the Bride's father an arm and a leg. Just as the driver was pulling away from the hotel entrance, a figure burst through the door and ran towards the taxi. Jumping in, he informed the driver "Just Drive!" "Where to?" enquired the cabby. "Anywhere. Just get me away from here." On enquiring the reason for this, the fare explained that he was a priest and had just officiated at a large wedding. After the meal, the wedding party were making the thank you speeches. When it came to the turn of the Groom, he made the usual acknowledgements. He then went into his inside jacket pocket and produced an envelope saying "In here are two plane tickets to the Bahamas, for the honeymoon, given to me by Uncle Bernie. "But I should really give them to the bride and best man as they have been shagging for the past six months." With that, he laid the envelope in front of the bride and walked out of the room amid cries of disbelief from the man's new wife, assembled guests, horror from the bride's mother and outrage from the best man's wife.

One warm summer's day Charlie picked up an American tourist to take him to the Castle. It was heavy traffic and they had all the windows open. They were stopped by a red light at a Pelican crossing which had recently had an automated voice installed warning pedestrians that the traffic heading towards Princes Street had stopped. "What's that voice?" asked the tourist. "It's talking traffic lights for blind people" replied Charlie. "It's telling them that the traffic light is red." "That's amazing!" responded the American. "Back home they don't allow blind people to drive."

Andy Sinclair, who used a motorbike to get to work, kept his crash helmet in the luggage compartment of the taxi.

Sitting on the rank one day, a business man came up to him and said "Airport, as fast as you can." Reaching for his helmet Andy said to the fare, "Fasten your seat belt and hold on," to which the deflated business man replied "I didn't mean that fast."

Derek and Bill were old friends and golfing partners who decided to go for a few days golf up north. Staying in a small hotel midweek they, got good rates. With wonderful weather and beautiful courses, they had a great time. On returning home, they were telling everyone on the rank how good the few days had been. Nine months later Bill received a letter from a lawyer in the town where they had stayed. On meeting Derek on the rank that night, Bill enquired if, on their break, had he slept with the landlady? "I sure did, and it was great!" replied Derek. "Did you use my name?" asked Bill. "Well, yes I did. How did you find out?" "Because this morning I got a letter from her lawyer informing me she had died and left me £20,000 as she could not forget our time together.

On a fishing trip a group of cabbies hired a boat. Loading it up with rods and reels, plenty of beer and sandwiches, they were all set for a day at sea.

By mid-afternoon the sky had clouded over, the wind had got up and there was a swell running. Peter began to feel unwell. He went to the rail, where he threw up, losing his false teeth in the process. He cursed what had happened, how much they had cost him and how was he going to explain it to his wife. This greatly amused the others in the group and they decided to play a trick on him. Going to the other side of the boat, one of them removed his false teeth and tying them to his rod, pretended to pull them from the sea. "Look at what I've caught!" he exclaimed. Peter went over to see. He unhooked them from the line, put them in his mouth for a second before removing them and threw them over the side with the words "They are not mine."

One Thursday night heading into town along the Corstorphine Road, a driver came across a police car blocking the road and diverting him onto a side street. Asking the policeman what was wrong, he was told to go about his business. On rejoining the main road, past the Zoo there was another road block, but looking along the road there was nothing to see. Later that night having a coffee at the garage he met John, whose company had the contract to take the staff home from the hotel next to the Zoo. He asked John if he knew what the cause of the road closure had been. John did and told him the story.

The night porter and the receptionist were having a quiet night and were watching Crime Watch on television. One of the items was about an armed robber named John Smith. Nick Ross showed a photo-fit of the man and advised the public not to have a go, but to call the police with his whereabouts. The night porter told the receptionist that the photo-fit was a dead ringer for the man staying in room 301. The receptionist checked the register and saw the name of John Smith, who had booked in for one night only and had paid cash in advance. Being very suspicious, they telephoned the police. When the police arrived, they closed the road and evacuated the rooms on either side of 301. Using pass keys, armed officers burst into the room and leapt on the man in bed, but he was not alone. He had a female companion.

Questioning him, he admitted that he used a false name and gave the police his address. They then sent a police car to the address to check if he was telling the truth. Getting the lady of the house out of bed, they asked her where her husband was and she replied that he was in London on business. They informed her that indeed that was not the case as he was in the Poste House on funny business.

Wee Bobby told the tale of attending his niece's wedding. It was a fancy affair and had been the talk of the family for almost a year. No expense was to be spared on the great day and it was to be the best wedding in the family history.

The future bride and groom met with the minister to discuss arrangements. They were informed that the church was taking a modern step and were allowing the happy couple to choose the music that the bride would walk down the aisle to. "It does not have to be the traditional Here comes the Bride" said the minister. "It can be anything that means something special to you." The Bride thought for a moment and said, "Could we have "Everything I do, I do it for you" by Bryan Adams?" "I don't think I know that one," replied the organist. "It's the theme from Robin Hood," said the bride, referring to the recent film starring Kevin Costner. "Oh, I know it!" said the elderly organist. The great day arrived. The church was full of family and friends in their finest outfits, and the children were on their best behaviour as they all waited for the arrival of the Bride. When the church doors opened, the organist broke into the tune "Robin Hood, Robin Hood, riding through the glen" which had been the signature tune to the television series of the 1950's.

One day I picked up a middle-aged lady from the George hotel who asked to go to Greenbank Drive. She was a typical overbearing type with more money than manners. During the journey, she said that she was on a visit to find her birth place. All she knew was that the address was Greenbank Drive and she had a number.

She had been told that she was born in a big house, most probably a stately home. Despite a careful search, we could not find the number. She started to question my ability as a taxi driver as I could not find the number and enquired if we were even in the right street. Pulling up at the house on the corner with Greenbank Terrace, I saw there was an old man in the garden. I asked him if he knew where this number could be and he told us that this was it. The lady told him that she had been born there. He went on to explain that the building used to be a gatehouse for the Craiglockart Poor House. To prevent any future stigma, all children born in the poor house had their births recorded at that address.

I took one subdued lady back to the George.

I received a radio job one Sunday afternoon to pick up a fare at the Accident and Emergency at the Western General Hospital. I arrived to find a teenage boy in a wheelchair, accompanied by a woman, who was obviously his mother. Getting out to help the young man into the cab, I was told, in a very brusque tone by the woman, that she did not need any help. As she got the young man into the cab, I returned the wheelchair to reception. As we set off, she gave me their destination, a sheltered housing complex for army veterans. On arrival at their house, the woman threw a five-pound note through the glass partition, then stormed out of the cab, leaving the young man to get himself out. Watching him struggle amid moans of pain, I went to his assistance. He was having great difficulty getting out of the seat, I practically had to lift him to get him out of the cab. While helping him, I noticed the front of his trousers were caked with dried blood and that his zipper was missing. Asking him what had happened, he told me that earlier that afternoon, he and his girlfriend were upstairs, messing about when they heard his mother coming up the stairs. The girlfriend panicked and quickly pulled up his zip, catching his wedding tackle. He had to go to the hospital to have the zipper removed before having the wound stitched. I have often wondered what became of their relationship. I can feel his pain.

Before the advent of plastic coin dispensers, taxi drivers used a wrist bag which was a leather pouch with a drawstring. This was useful in three ways, not only did it hold all your coins, it also helped the customer to identify you as a taxi driver when going into licensed premises, and it could be used as a means of defence in the event of an attempted assault. The best place to buy one was a small leather shop on Lauriston Street, run by Ludwik Jaszczur. Ludwik was a Polish gentleman, who after WWII, like so many of his countrymen, decided to stay in Scotland. They were very friendly and hard-working people. When starting as a taxi driver, the older drivers told me where to go to buy a cash bag. When I went to the shop to buy one, "The Pole," as he was known to the trade, asked me if I knew John Graves. (V71) When I told him I did, he asked to be remembered to him. He then went on to tell me that he used to be a typewriter mechanic alongside John. As he could not speak very good English, John would help him by filling in their time sheets. With a twinkle in his eye, he said he had never had so much money, thanks to John and his creative accounting. Ludwik, well into his 90's, retired in 2019.His daughter ran the business until covid 19 sadly forced its closure.

One warm and sunny day, with not very much happening, I picked up a fare from the Waverley Station. The fare was dressed in a three-piece suit, with a pocket watch on a chain with a fob and a handkerchief displayed very flamboyantly in his top pocket. In a very well-modulated voice, he asked to be taken to the Sheriff Court. During the journey he passed the comment that it was a damn shame that he would be in court all day when he could be on the golf course. I said, "If you plead guilty straight away, you might get bail." He exploded from the seat and in a very outraged voice shouted, "I'm a lawyer, not a defendant!" Obviously, it was a bare fare with no tip.

At the height of the AIDS epidemic, I picked up two young men one night. They were no sooner in the cab when they started to kiss and fondle each other.

As things were getting a bit serious, I asked them to stop, which they did for a few minutes, but soon started again, with renewed passion. I again asked them to stop and told them to wait until they got home, or I would ask them to get out of the cab. They sat apart for a few minutes then they started undoing each other's trousers. This for me was the final straw. I pulled over, stopped the cab and put them out. My next fare was a young lady, who handed me a box and told me she had found it on the floor of the cab. Realizing it must have belonged to the two young men, I put it in the luggage compartment and forgot about it. A few days later, I opened the box and found a 200ml bottle of Paco Rabanne gents toilette spray. I had never heard of the brand but found the perfume quite pleasant. Giving myself a quick spray, I went to City Cabs garage to pay my radio dues. Standing in the queue chatting to other drivers, someone came close and giving a sniff, said to me, "God Almighty! What have you got on? You smell like a poof!" Knowing where it came from, I immediately when to the toilet and washed my face before throwing the bottle in the bucket. It was only later that I discovered that it was a very expensive brand.

As taxi driving is a second vocation, it stands to reason that drivers had other jobs before joining the trade. One such man was employed by Scottish Power as a technician whose job was to go to premises that were experiencing problems. Starting work one morning, he was dispatched to a house where the lady householder was in a panic. She thought her electric meter was about to explode as it was making a buzzing sound. When the technician arrived, he managed to calm the lady down before going to check the meter which was housed in a cupboard. When he opened the cupboard door, he could hear a definite buzzing sound which didn't seem to be coming from the meter, but rather, through the wall. Asking the lady what was behind the wall, the lady told him it was her daughter's bedroom. Going into the bedroom to investigate, he saw a bedside cabinet against the wall which seemed to be making a noise. Opening the drawer, he found a vibrator which had been left switched on. Problem solved, much to the lady's embarrassment.

Today, Mary King's Close, underneath the City Chambers, is one of the top tourist attractions on the Royal Mile, but this was not always the case. For many years the close was only open to visitors with a special guide. Only two men were allowed to take the tours down, one being Councillor Wilson and the other was Bill McKelvie of the Festival Guides Association. Arranging a tour with Bill McKelvie, a group of taxi drivers met in the quadrangle and had to go into the City Chambers to gain access. This was achieved by opening a trapdoor in the floor and descending a ladder. The council official who led the party in, warned that no photography was allowed, as the flash could cause damage to the walls. (I still can't believe that!) One of the party, Dougie Lamb, had a camera with him. As it wasn't allowed, he put it in his inside jacket pocket and zipped it up so no one could see it. At the end of the tour, as the taxi drivers were leaving one of the rooms, another group, led by Councillor Wilson, was entering. It was quite dark, the only light being a couple of 40 watt light bulbs. Councillor Wilson started his spiel and our group stopped to listen. He was telling them that one night he took a tour down with a head count of 16 people in, and 15 people out. This shows that his mastery of arithmetic leaves a lot to be desired. He then went on to relate a story in which he said that during one tour, a woman noticed a small girl sitting against the wall crying. The woman went over to the girl, who said her name was Annie. The woman offered Annie a packet of sweets. Taking the sweets, Annie then stood up in a bright light and walked through the wall. At this point, Councillor Wilson's audience was transfixed. Then Dougie Lamb turned his back on the group and unzipped his jacket pocket, pressed the flash button on his camera, causing a blinding flash. There was a great deal of consternation among the group amid loud cries of "We have seen a ghost!" The taxi drivers were trying to suppress their laughter as they left to adjourn to the pub, where they were able to laugh freely. When the attraction was opened to the public, a group of City Guides were invited to a tour so that they could tell tourist that it was worth a visit. Imagine the surprise we had when the young girl who was acting as a guide, started to relate the story of when Councillor Wilson led a party who were blinded by a bright light and a ghost appeared. We tried to tell her it was Dougie Lamb with his camera, but she was having none of it. So that is how legends are started.

Sometimes the lure of money overcomes common sense.

One Christmas Day, Wee Bobby Shennan went into the Waverley Station to use the toilet. On rejoining his cab, a young lady approached him and enquired if he was available to take her to London, as there were no trains running across the border. She explained that it was imperative that she be in London that evening and the only way to get there was by taxi. She further explained that she had no money, but her boyfriend would pay when they reached London. She produced the phone number of her boyfriend and asked Bobby to call him to verify her story. Bobby made the call and the man on the other end asked how much the fare would be. When this was agreed to, the man told Bobby to bring her to an address and he would pay the fare. Bobby then phoned his nightshift driver, explained the arrangements and asked him to accompany them so that the driving could be shared. They set off mid-morning, with Bobby and his driver taking spells behind the wheel. En route, they stopped for a break and something to eat. (Paid for by Bobby) During the break, Bobby again phoned the number he had been given, which again was answered by the boyfriend, who reassured Bobby that his money was safe and enquired what time they would arrive. Encouraged that all was well, the trio set off. Arriving at the address, which turned out to be a pub which was closed, Bobby called the phone number of the boyfriend, but it went unanswered. The young lady said she had no idea where he was and after a period of time it was apparent that no one was going to pay. Bobby took the young lady to the Police Station and explained the situation to the Desk Officer. Bobby was shocked when he explained there was nothing the Police could do as the young lady had told Bobby that she had no money before they had left Edinburgh. The arrangement for payment was with someone unknown. So, it was two very chastened cabbies that made the journey home. Not only had they missed out on one of the most lucrative days of the year, they were also out of pocket for the cost of diesel and food.

Sitting third on the Waverley Bridge rank one night, I watched as a young man approached the first cab and spoke to the driver. He then went to the second cab and spoke to that driver too before approaching me. He asked to go to Brighton and said he would pay by cheque. There was no way that was going to happen. When the other two drivers who had also declined the fare joined us and we explained that it would be quicker and less expensive to go to a cheap Bed and Breakfast, go to the Airport in the morning, take the first flight to Gatwick and then get a taxi to his destination. He was having none of it. Going to the fourth cab, which was driven by a comparatively new driver, he asked him. Blinded by the thought of a large fare, and despite warnings from more experienced drivers, they set off. Taking about ten hours to drive down, including rest breaks, the driver phoned his boss and explained where he was and said he would not be back until around8pm. On arrival in Brighton, the fare gave the driver what the driver assumed was a cheque, but in fact it was a 'pay in slip' from a cheque book.

On arrival back in Edinburgh, he found out he had been duped. To add insult to injury, he had to cover his boss's loss of earnings for the day. Taking into account his loss of earnings for two nights, food and fuel for the journey plus his boss's loss of earnings, it was a very costly experience. The night shift drivers were not at all sympathetic to his plight and he quickly became known as "The Brighton Belle."

When Scotland played Ireland at rugby, big Grant picked up an Irishman around midnight. When taking him to his hotel, Paddy asked if they could stop at a garage so he could buy some cigarettes. Pulling onto the forecourt and stopping at the kiosk, Grant informed the Irishman, "It's past midnight, so you will have to use the window as the door is locked for security reasons." Hearing strange sounds from the back of the cab, Grant turned around to find the Irishman halfway through the nearside passenger window, before falling in a heap in front of a bewildered attendant. "What the hell are you doing?" demanded Grant. Paddy replied, "You said to use the window as the door is locked."

During a rugby international weekend, when Scotland were playing Wales, the tickets were in high demand. Wee Willie Gordon, better known as the Poison Dwarf, picked up five Welshmen and got the usual question "Got any tickets?" "Yes." was the reply, "I have two." "We need three," replied Dai. Proceeding to the stadium down Lothian Road, they were stopped by traffic lights at Princes Street. Whilst sitting in the middle lane, a hearse pulled up in the outside lane. Wee Willie heard banging coming from behind and turned around to see a Welshman leaning out the window and tapping on the window of the hearse, nodding at the coffin and asking the minister "Did he have a ticket for the match?"

"Skoogs" picked up a man who was a bit the worse for wear. They were almost at his house, when he heard the sound that terrifies all taxi drivers, the sound of someone retching. By the time he pulled over the man had been sick on the floor. "Sorry about that son. It must have been something I ate." (Nothing to do with the eighteen pints of lager) "But don't worry about it as I will clean it up. Drive round the corner to my house and I will get a bucket of water and some disinfectant." While the fare went indoors, Skoogs opened both passenger doors and the man came back carrying a basin full of water. "Just throw it on the floor" ordered Skoogs, and the man obliged. There followed an almighty crash and when they checked the back of the cab they found it covered in broken cups and plates, knives, forks and spoons. The man had gone into the kitchen for water and seeing the basin full, thought, "That's handy" but was too drunk to notice the contents.

Not everybody is suitable to drive taxis as the stress can sometimes be overpowering.

Alec, who was a postman, but to earn extra cash, passed his test and worked for P52 on Monday, Wednesday and Friday nights. One glorious sunny evening in July, he went into the Waverley Station where he was flagged down by a station porter, whom he knew, and was asked if he wanted a fare to St. Andrews. Most definitely! Taking him round to the Station Master's office, the porter pointed out four Japanese gentlemen. "That's them" he said and proceeded to help put their luggage into the cab. Alec asked where they were going and received the reply "We go St. Andrews." So off they set. Arriving in St. Andrews, Alec asked them the name of their hotel and received the reply "We go St. Andrews." Realizing that they did not speak English, Alec again attempted to find out which hotel they were staying. Again, the reply was "We go St. Andrews." Alec attempted to explain that this was St. Andrews. They smiled and nodded, "Ok we go St. Andrews hotel."

A sudden panic attack struck Alec, who knew that the St. Andrews hotel was on South St. Andrew Street. Trying to make himself understood, Alec said "St. Andrews! Golf! Tommy Nakajima!" Quizzical looks appeared on their faces, then a look of understanding. Tommy Nakajima was a Japanese golfer, who in the 1978 Open at St. Andrews while sharing the lead, was on the 17th green in two. He then proceeded to putt into the road hole bunker, take four shots to get out and card a nine, ending his hopes of the championship. The whole episode was being shown live on T.V. around the world. The party got all excited so Alec, with nothing to lose took them to the side of the 18th fairway and parked the cab. He took them to the 17th Green, where they had their photos taken and again on the Swilken Bridge. Returning to Edinburgh and pulling up at St. Andrews hotel, they were met by other members of their party who asked where they had been. One of the group, who could speak English, asked Alec what happened.

After getting an explanation, the man turned to the others and asked them what happened. After a very long speech in Japanese, with much smiling and nodding heads, the interpreter turned to Alec and told him that his friends had enjoyed a very memorable outing. He explained that they had seen things they could not have imagined, and as they followed golf on TV, they had seen the incident. When asked how much the fare was, Alec was put in a quandary. How could he charge them? However, he had put the meter on and it was running the whole time. The Japanese gentleman saw this and told his friends. They agreed to pay what was on the meter, plus a tip, as Alec had been so kind. After saying goodbye to his new friends, Alec drove to his owner's house and handed in the keys "Saying this job is not for me" and never drove a taxi again.

A number of years ago my son Neil and I were invited on Liverpool Blind Kids Outing.

After a visit to London, where a large number of idiots had St. Georges flags attached to their windows, we decided to show a bit of class.

Going to a scrappy we got two sets of scrapped wheel trims. Spraying them blue we put white tape on to represent the Saltire. Neil attached them using cheap cable ties. The result being, by the time we got to Liverpool, we each had lost the front and rear nearside trims. On arriving, we phoned Dave to ask for directions to our accommodation and as a joke we said "We have only been here five bloody minutes and already they have stolen our wheel trims."

"You are joking!" he responded. "No, we are not! You will see for yourself when we arrive at the Twelfth Man," which was the pub we were staying in overnight. Explaining what happened, we said that we were stopped at traffic lights outside the Windsor pub, when a group of youths ran forward shouting "We will have them!" and whipped the wheel trims off. A Liverpool cabbie asked why we did not have them cable tied on, when Sheldon Collins, a London cabbie who was on the trip, and nowhere near the alleged incident said "Little bastards had a Stanley knife, didn't they?" To which we had to agree. We went into the bar with Sheldon for a drink, obviously we were paying, as Sheldon is one of God's chosen people. Later that night the organizer of the outing came into the bar with a box. Handing it to me, he told us that they had a whip round on the ranks and raised money to buy a new set of wheel trims. Now what could we do? The best thing was to keep stum.

The next morning while decorating our cabs, we replaced the missing wheel trims with the already painted spares from the boot. On arrival at the Blind School, we were waiting on the kids when a young lady approached and asked if we were the Edinburgh cabbies. She was a reporter from the Liverpool Echo and was covering the outing. She asked if it was true that we had our wheel trims stolen, and we agreed. On returning from the outing we were shown the paper where, on the front page was the headline

EDINBURGH CABBIES ON CHARITY
TRIP GET WHEEL TRIMS STOLEN

Now the sad part of this story is that at no time was our story questioned and I don't really want to go back to Scouse Land.

When Princess Margaret, Diana, the Princess of Wales and Sarah Ferguson attended a banquet in the Palace of Holyrood House, ten taxis were required to take home the catering staff after the event. The taxis were instructed to wait in Abbey Strand and not to enter the palace grounds.

The taxis were all lined up outside the gates when the last car arrived, driven by Crazy Pony, younger brother of Crazy Horse. He pulled up alongside the first car where all the drivers had congregated for a blether and asked "What are you waiting here for?" "That's what we have been told to do" was the answer. Now Crazy Pony was not known for his patience, "F*ck that!" was his response. "I will sort them out" and he drove through the gates heading for the main entrance to shouts of encouragement from the assembled drivers. Pulling up at the main entrance, the taxi had hardly stopped when a soldier yanked the door open and grabbing Pony by the scruff of the neck, threw him down on the ground with an Sa 80 pointed at his head. All of this to shouts from the cabbies, "Shoot the bastard! He's a nutter" Happy Days.

In the days of voice radio, the procedure was
    1st Call = in the street
    2nd Call = in the vicinity
    3rd Call = acceptance, ie any car, anywhere

The nearest car to the job got it. Locations were measured in the control room with a piece of string, (rumoured on the ranks to be a length of elastic.) This gave rise to what became known as 'siver man,' someone who would appear nearer than anybody when the job was being measured.

There were a few regulars who the drivers knew by first name and would go the extra mile for them as they were good tippers. These people never had a problem getting a cab no matter how busy, all the controller had to say was "Its for"....., give the name, and cabs would be trying to claim the job from all over. One such man was Ian MacDonald, who lived with his mother in a bungalow on Inverleith Row, opposite what was then the Marina hotel. He was a millionaire and was a descendant of MacDonald & Muir, whisky distillers. He owned various pubs in town like the Grey Horse on Dalkeith Road and had a large portfolio of property in Glasgow. As well as this he had two yachts which he chartered out in the Caribbean. He lost his driving licence due to drink driving, left his top of the range Jaguar in his driveway and thereafter used taxis. If you were lucky enough to get him as a fare, that was you finished for the day. He never paid any heed to what was on the meter, he would ask the driver how much he wanted and that was what you got.

Many drivers, myself included, didn't always put the meter on when you had him as a fare. One Saturday evening when dropping off at the Carlton hotel, I heard "1st Call, the Black Swan." (now Albanach) As City Cabs never took work from licensed premises it was worth a shout getting the job. I was told "Pick up Ian MacDonald, - going somewhere." Parking the taxi at the top of Cockburn Street, I went into the pub and found Ian, telling him I was outside whenever he was ready. He turned to the barman and said, "Told you." The barman went into the till and took out a £5 note, gave it to Ian who gave it to me and said to me "I bet him a fiver I could get a taxi inside five minutes."

Ian would use taxis when visiting his businesses or when trying to track down a business acquaintance. It was never just A to B. Each time he got out of the cab, he would give the driver £5 saying "I will be back in a few minutes." Tonight, was no exception. "Take me to the George Hotel, I left my coat there earlier" he said. Arriving at the George, he gave me £5 and asked me to go and get his coat from the lounge as he did not want to get involved with the company again. I retrieved his coat and returned it to him. He checked the inside pocket and said "Oh good! It's still there" and produced a A5 size envelope stuffed full of cash. "Now take me to the Stags Head, I need to see a man." Arriving at the pub, he gave me £5 and said, "I will only be a few minutes." Getting out of the car, he went into the pub only to return a few minutes later saying "He's not in there. Take me to MacGlaughlins." (across the road). The same procedure took place, he gave me £5 and went inside. The door had hardly swung shut when he reappeared, saying "He is not in there, let's try the Northern." Arriving at the Northern he gave me another £5 and said, "I will see if he is there, if not, take me to the Forth Corinthian Yacht Club."

He returned a few minutes later to tell me that he had found him and giving me £5 he told me to come back in an hour and to keep the meter running.

I went to City Cabs garage on East London Street, washed the cab and had a cup of coffee. After an hour I went back to the Northern Bar. Going inside, I informed Ian I was back, and this time, he gave me £10 and said his business was not yet finished so I went back to the taxi to wait. After ten minutes he appeared, gave me £10 saying he was sorry to keep me waiting but would not be long. This was repeated a further four times. When he finally appeared. I said "Down to the yacht club Ian?" "Nah, I've had enough! Sorry for messing you about." He then gave me another £10 and said, "Take me home."

Pulling up at his house at around half past seven, he asked what was on the meter. I said "£35." Producing a coin, he asked "Do you want to do double or quits?" "Ok" I said "Heads." He tossed the coin and up came heads. "Well done! Do you want to do another double or quits?" Again, I said heads and again he tossed the coin and up came heads again. "You are on a roll. Double or quits?" This time I said to him, "Ian, I have a young family and cannot afford to gamble £140.""Very sensible," he said and produced the cash. "I will make it £150 as we have had a good laugh." Giving me the money, he asked how many kids I had, I told him two (I should have said four) and he handed me two twenty-pound notes, "Buy them a present from me." While Ian was still in the cab, a taxi pulled up behind me and Willie Neil (V144) known as Aberdeen Angus got out and came forward for a chat. As we were talking, an airport taxi pulled up at the Marina hotel and the fare got out carrying a set of golf clubs and a suit case. He went into the hotel and came out a few minutes later and crossing over to us enquired if we were free. Willie said he was booked on a job, but I told him I was free, said cheerio to Ian and the guy got in the cab. When I asked the man where he wanted to go, he said

"Marine Hotel, North Berwick. Stupid driver took me to the wrong hotel." The fare turned out to be Seve Ballesteros, going to play in a competition.

Back in town and after stopping for supper, I started to work around 10.30pm, finishing at about 5am.

As it was the end of the shift I went to the garage and met up with some of the other drivers. I was surprised to find that I was not the top earner. Two other drivers who had never left town had £50-60 more than me. Moral of the story is - never to believe what a taxi driver tells you he earns.

At Kerlin Taxi School a student named Yvonne Rodden was due to sit her topographical test but despite reassurances that she would pass, was overcome with nerves.

One evening she came to the school all excited, she had sat her test that morning and had passed. Jimmy Kerlin asked her how she had coped with her nerves and she produced a spray she had purchased from Napiers the herbalist. She told us that a couple of squirts on to the tongue and everything was cool.

Another student, an Asian man who was due to sit his test in two days' time asked her how much it cost. "£4.99" was the reply. He explained that he was nervous and would maybe try it. Now to be fair, an Asian man will not willingly spend unnecessary cash, so he went to his brother who was a doctor and asked for something to calm him down. His brother gave him some pills and told him to take one an hour before sitting the test.

The evening after his test he came to the school to tell us that he had passed. Jimmy asked him how he coped with his nerves and he told us about the pills. Waking up in the morning, he took a pill (just to make sure it worked) but it didn't, so an hour later he took another one but that did not work either. By mid-morning he was getting desperate so took another one. Then just before sitting the test he took another pill. When the examination started, he picked up his paper and started to read through it as Jimmy had told him. Looking over the paper he said to himself "I know that" next question "I know that" and so on until he reached the end but he was not writing down the answers. Completely relaxed, he started to fill in the answers. After a short while the adjudicator told them that there was 15 minutes left. He had not yet started on his routes. As he hurriedly filled in the routes he wrote on the paper "PLEASE EXCUSE MY HAND WRITING.AT THIS POINT I PANICKED." Trying to keep a straight face, Jimmy looked very serious and told him "I wish you hadn't told us that, but now I am duty bound to inform the cab office that you sat the test under the influence of drugs, and they will revoke your licence." Cue Asian man swallowing the remainder of the pills.

Wee Jimmy Craig was not known for his sartorial elegance, in fact, dressed in a Gucci suit, he would still look like an unmade bed. A point proved one day when he got a job from Jericho House, on the corner of Bristo Place and Lothian Street. The building was run by the Benedictine order of monks and they gave succour to the homeless. When Wee Jimmy rang the bell to announce his arrival, a monk opened the door, took a look at him and asked him to wait a minute. A couple of minutes later the brother opened the door and gave Jimmy a bag containing sandwiches as he thought he was homeless. Now as sad as this may seem, it's not as sad as the fact Jimmy took the sandwiches.

I passed the topographical test in January 1979 and started work on day shift V9. It was a really bad winter with the road gritters on strike and no buses running. Going into the Waverley Station, the queue was around the block. The Railway Police, who were marshalling the rank, asked the first person where they are going. "Gilmerton." was the reply. The Railway Police then went down the queue, asking anybody going south to share the taxi. At various stops passengers paid what was on the meter. Happy days and no complaints. People were just glad to get home.

As I was just out the wrapper and inexperienced, I thought this was the best job ever. One morning while in

Corstorphine High Street, over the radio came a call "1st call north of the bridge." No cars responded. "2nd call north of the bridge." No cars responded. "3rd call north of the bridge." I just about dropped the mike with excitement. I gave my location and got the job to pick up a parcel in Ardersier and take it to Sale in Greater Manchester. The job was contract to I.B.M. Thinking I had won the prize, I set off. No motorways and the roads were barely passable. Only later I found out no other cab had claimed the job because of the road conditions. Picking up the part, (a small envelope which fitted in my pocket) I started to head south, stopping for fuel at the services at the Forth Bridge. As it was approaching change over time, I phoned Joe and told him I would be at his house in 20 minutes and that he had a part going to Sale. His first response was "Where is that?" When I told him, he told me just to complete the job myself.

I phoned home and asked my wife to get a meal ready and a flask of coffee. I set off for Manchester and on the way, I saw lorries in lay- by's with fires underneath them. The drivers were trying to thaw out their diesel tanks.

Seeing the sign for Sale, I pulled off the motorway and drove along with not a clue as to where I was going. I spotted a Royal Mail van and asked the driver where the Industrial Estate was. He replied, "It's a bit complicated, but follow me." After about 20 minutes he pulled up at the entrance to an Industrial Estate and waited while I gave the parcel to the security guard. He then showed me the way back to the motorway. It was definitely worth the fiver I slipped him. Now it was head for home. Coming back into town at 7am. and approaching Fairmilehead, I called control to notify them I had completed the job. She asked my location and when I told her, she gave me a job from the P.M.R. going to the Western General. When I refused it she put me on report for refusing a contract job. A bit harsh, as I had only been working for 26 hours. After going home for breakfast and a shower, I went to Joe's house at 9am, giving him the credit slip to take to the accounts office where he would get an instant pay out. He asked if I was not working and if not, he would work a day shift and pick me up about 5pm. and I could get a few hours in. The deal then was a 60/40 split with country work 50/50 less the fuel. The country jobs then were £1.20 a mile. When Joe came to pick me up he handed me an envelope containing the full amount for the job. Querying this, his response was, "You did the job, you keep the cash." I never knew another owner to do this. As a post script to this story, a couple of days later I was at the garage and was asked how I got on with the job and telling them how I did it. Next day Kenny Jeffries (V67) got the same job, no problem to him, as I had marked his card. All was going well. He dropped the part off and was heading home. Not sure of the way he stopped at a service station where he saw an articulated lorry with the logo of a carrier from Blairgowrie. Thinking, I will follow him, and off they set. After 2 hours of driving Kenny thought, I should be heading north. The sun rises in the east, so why is it shining in my eyes? He found out shortly when he saw a sign 'Hull 5 miles' The lorry was heading for the ferry and Kenny was further away from home than when he started.

In City Cabs garage on East London street, was the "Howf," a place where drivers could go and vent their anger and frustrations at the public, committee and controllers. It was also a place where characters were assassinated, social events were planned and rumours started.

Tommy King asked in the Howf one night if anyone had seen the advert in the Scotsman newspaper requiring drivers to deliver 20 refuse lorries which Edinburgh Council had sold to a town in Spain. Tommy told us he was in with a shout to get the contract. A few days later he announced he had been successful, and they were sending out the details and he required drivers. Now Tommy had a lot of new 'friends' eager to buy him coffee in the hope he would choose them. After much discussion, it was decided that he would need a minimum of 30 drivers, to allow for change over. The Spanish Government were paying a daily wage plus food, ferry charges and fuel.

On arrival in Spain, the drivers would be put up in a hotel for a week and then flown back to Edinburgh. In next to no time Tommy had his drivers.

This started a rush to get passports, holidays booked, some even sitting their HGV. Each night in the howf the plan was gone over, ironing out the details such as, where the fuel and rest stops would be. It was decided, as they were accustomed to driving at night, this is when they would travel, taking two nights to drive to Portsmouth where they would board the ferry for Spain. Each night a different problem was discussed, and solutions found. Everybody on the list was getting excited as the time for departure drew near until Tommy called a final meeting where he asked the drivers to check what date it was. It turns out it was the 1st of April. Some of the drivers refused to believe it was a wind up and thought Tommy was only pretending it was a joke. It provided entertainment for the night shift for a few weeks. Moral of the story is. If it sounds too good to be true, it probably is.

Before becoming a taxi driver Bob Cummings (The Bear) led an interesting life. Living as a kaftan wearing hippie with flowers in his hair Bob was forcefully ejected from Majorca along with hundreds of others by General Franco.

This image is somewhat at odds with the short tempered taxi driver with a low level of tolerance to anyone who upset him.

Whilst cleaning the house one day the vacuum cleaner started to play up, cutting out then restarting, this went on for several minutes before cutting out completely. Bob decided to get someone in to fix the problem.

Next day the repair man arrived and had a quick look at it. Turning to Bob he said "Do you want me to get it running again?" "Of course, its no bloody good unless it is". replied Bob "Well" said the repair man "It will be £20 call out charge and £30 for the repair, a total of £50 cash up front". Bob going for his wallet, thought it a bit strange and a funny way of doing business. He handed over the money to the repair man who picked up his bag of tools before going over to the wall and giving the plug a kick into the socket. The vacuum started straight away and the repair man bolted before the Bear could grab him.

In the 1980's a group of taxi drivers from all the companies got together and arranged visits to interesting sites. These were held twice a month on Tuesday evenings. The places visited were many and varied including the Zoo, the Post Office Sorting Office, the Signalling Centre at Waverley, (where Bob Cummings (V89) controlled a London train from the border bridge to Waverley and went into a rant because a driver was not going fast enough), the Police H.Q., the Scottish War Memorial and various churches. This was always followed by a visit to licensed premises. One regular on these trips was Ronnie Tait, who when asked why he came on the outing replied, "It keeps me out the pub for a wee while." The nights out became known as "Keep Ronnie Tait Out The Pub Club."

On an organized tour of what was then Police H.Q. at Fettes, a group of taxi drivers were shown the control room and the forensic department, where one of the technicians explained finger printing and various other crime detection methods. Turning to credit card fraud, he explained how criminals stole credit cards and changed the signature on the back of the card into their own hand writing. Picking up a demonstration card he asked Wee Ronnie to sign the back. He then produced a bottle containing liquid. Dipping a cotton bud into the liquid, he proceeded to wipe the solution on the card and the signature disappeared without damaging the card. The criminal could then enter the signature in their own hand writing, all very impressive. Alec Cadden asked the technician what the liquid was, and he told us that it's a mixture of Coca Cola and brake fluid. Then Cadden asked "How much Coca Cola to how much brake fluid?" The technician started to tell us then stopped, saying "That's a secret." But we nearly found out.

During a visit to City observatory on Calton Hill, the astronomer was telling us about the history of the building and as it was such a clear evening, he invited us to go upstairs where he would open the roof and let us have a look through a telescope. Climbing up the spiral staircase we entered the inside of the dome. The guide was explaining how in days gone by, the roof was opened by pulling a chain, but nowadays it was by an electric motor. Starting it up, the roof started revolving, just as the last of the group were climbing the staircase. The last one up was wee Ronnie Tait, who was well known for his fondness for a drop or two or three or four. Upon reaching the upper level he looked up in amazement as the roof revolved. Alec Cadden, quick as a flash said "It's ok Ronnie. The roof really is spinning."

When the Whisky Heritage centre opened, the manager got in touch with me and asked if any taxi drivers in the tour group would be interested in a visit to this new attraction, with the view that they could steer visitors into the experience. Meeting in the Ensign Ewart pub, we made our way up to the Heritage centre where a young lady explained all about it. We were given a tour of the facility and then invited into a room in which a buffet had been laid on. After a short welcoming talk, the manager asked the young lady to bring a decanter of whisky. Giving all of us a commemorative glass, she started to pour each person a drink. Her first mistake was starting with wee Ronnie Tait. By the time she poured the party a drink, Ronnie had finished his, so she started again. When the decanter was finished the manager told her to bring another and the procedure was the same. In next to no time the decanter was emptied, and the manager told her to fetch another. This was repeated a further seven times before the manager threw up his hands in surrender and said "For God's sake! You are drinking it faster than we can make it."A memorable night.I was made an ambassador for the attraction and given a card which entitles me to a glass of whisky whenever I produced it. I asked how long it was valid for and I was told 'For life.' Then I asked how often it could be used and was told as often as I liked. "What, every day?" I asked. "Yes, that would be ok," was the answer. I tried to buy a house on Castle Hill but was outbid.

Sometimes you just can't win. Bad tempered cabbie Colin was driving down Dundas Street when he saw a cat get run over by a car which did not stop. Doing the right thing, he pulled over and tried to comfort the animal. Realising it needed the attention of a vet, he contacted control to call one out. When the vet arrived, Colin took the cat to him and the vet treated the animal. He then proceeded to present Colin with a bill. Colin explained that it was not his cat, but the vet told him "You called me out. You have to pay." £30 lighter, Colin went to the howf to share his tale of woe but was met with "Silly bugger! You should have let it die." A few weeks later while sitting at traffic lights at Jocks Lodge, he witnessed a cat running across the road. A car coming from Willowbrae Road ran over it and did not stop. With the cat lying in the middle of the road and howling in agony, Colin thought I will not get caught again and when the lights changed, he manoeuvred the cab so that he would run it over and put it out of its misery. This he did and drove on. However, a member of the public had noticed what he had done and took down his number and reported him to the police. He was charged and fined £40. When he came to the howf and related the tale, he got no sympathy but was greeted with gales of laughter.

Now in his 70's, ex owner and now driving night shift on V 36, Davie Purves had seen it all and done it all. One evening he picked up four youths going to Giro City. (Niddry) Going along Peffermill Road, they asked him to stop as one of them was getting out while the others were carrying on. No sooner had Davie stopped, than both doors opened and the four jumped out and ran away up the road. Stopping about a hundred yards away they started to taunt Davie with cries of "Come on granddad! Fight for your cash" and similar invitations to have sex with himself. As they had left both doors open, Davie got out to close them, when he noticed an electric guitar on the floor. Going back to the driver's seat, amid more cries to fight, he held up the guitar and shouted, "Is this yours?" Now there was panic amongst the yobs. "Oh, wait a minute driver. How much is the fare?" they asked as they started walking back towards the cab. "Don't bother, bastards! I don't want it." Davie then placed the guitar under the back wheel of the cab, jumped in and drove over it. He then proceeded back into town well satisfied.

Despite police enquiries the driver was never traced.

One evening Auld Tam (V153) came into the howf and was in his usual bad mood. When asked who had upset him he explained that the job was getting worse. "You pick up more dirt than a scaffie's barrow." When asked to elaborate, he explained that he picked up a man going to Blackford Glen Road. Turning into the road, Tam asked where about he should stop. The fare told him to keep driving. Now Tam knew that the houses were only for a short distance and then the road ran down into a council yard where there was no street lighting, but the fare kept telling him to keep going. Tam, thinking he was going to be robbed, was trying to get the fire extinguisher unhooked to use as a weapon to defend himself. He decided to go no further, despite the fare's insistence. Asking the fare why he wanted to go down there as there was nothing down there, the fare produced a leather belt and said "I will give you £25 to spank me." We looked at Tam and asked, "What did you do?" "Threw the dirty bastard out, didn't I?" "Well" said Skoogs "It's been a quiet Tuesday night. For £25, I wouldn't have spanked him, I would have kicked the shit out of him."

Getting a radio job from the Barnton hotel to pick up Mr. Wilson turned out to be one of the strangest jobs I ever had. Going into the reception to announce my arrival, I was greeted with "Thank God you're here. I will get your fare." Returning to the cab to wait, I was surprised to see the manager escorting a man from the premises who was wearing an ankle length overcoat, a Glengarry and carrying a shepherd's crook. The manager opened the door, ushered the man in and told me to take him away. He has got money, he added. Asking the man for a destination he told me R.B.S. Queensferry High Street. As we were driving along, he kept bursting into fits of giggles. Asking him to share the joke, he told me that he wanted lunch at the hotel, but the staff would not serve him. He was asked to leave as they would get complaints from the other customers. Still giggling he told me "I got the devils back though." "How did you manage that?" I asked. "You got thrown out." This produced another fit of giggles and going into the inside pocket of his overcoat he started to produce about 15 cruet sets. "I only took all these. See if they get complaints now," he replied. Arriving at the bank, he left his shepherd's crook and told me to wait as he may be a while. He then went into the bank. After about 40 minutes I started to get a bit worried and went into the bank to enquire how much longer he would be, and to my surprise the teller told me he was having a cup of tea with the manager. He said not to worry as he would not be much longer. After another 20 minutes Mr. Wilson came back and told me that everything is settled now and to take him to Gleneagles Hotel. Quoting him a price, plus what was on the meter, I asked for cash up front. He replied with "Very sensible driver. You never know who you are dealing with these days. The world is full of bampots." 'Aye, and you're one of them' I thought, as he produced a wad of £20 notes. So, we set off for Gleneagles. "I have been told you get a nice lunch there," was the only comment he made on the journey. Arriving at the hotel, the concierge came and opened the door for him and getting out, he started to do a jig going up the stairs. The concierge looked at me aghast and I just shrugged my shoulders. Pulling away, I realized he had left his shepherd's crook in the back of the taxi. Going into the hotel, I met the concierge who told me to wait until Mr. Wilson had lunch and then take him back to Edinburgh. While I was waiting, I was to be provided with some sandwiches and coffee which would be paid for by Mr. Wilson. That will do for me, I thought and settled down to wait. After a couple of hours Mr. Wilson returned and enquired if I had a satisfactory lunch, and if so, we should go to the Roxburgh Hotel.

Again he produced his wad of cash and asked me how much I wanted. Arriving at the Roxburgh, he got out and went to the near side window. He said he had enjoyed a wonderful day, then asked me if I was married. He threw a £20 note into the luggage compartment and told me to buy my wife a present. He asked if I had kids, then proceeded to throw £20 notes through the window, all the time giggling like mad. I was starting to get a bit concerned when the porter came out and greeted him like an old friend. Picking up the notes, I was trying to explain to the porter what the score was, but he just shook his head and said "It's ok. He likes you. Just keep the money. He is a regular here. He lives in Moray Place." Then, to get rid of me, asked "Will you take a job to the airport?'

The end of a memorable shift.

The contract City Cabs had with I.B.M. was one of the jewels in their crown.

Money was no object when it came to getting parts to anywhere in the country and the frequency they used cabs was almost beyond belief. It was not unknown for six or seven cabs to go to Spango Valley in Greenock in a day. Some of the more memorable jobs went to London. One night, Dougie Brown was on the Waverley Bridge rank when he got a job to take a small parcel from I.B.M. stores in St. Andrew Square to go to London. Now Dougie was a smart cookie. He collected the part and drove into Waverley station where he parked the cab in the free car park and boarded the sleeper train. Arriving in London, he took a cab to the industrial estate where he met the I.B.M. engineer and handed the part over. He then took a tube train to Heathrow, got on a flight to Edinburgh where he took the airport bus to Waverley Bridge, picked up his cab and ranked on the East. Now there was hell to pay. How could he have done the job in under 12 hours when it would have taken 10 hours to drive to London? He was put on report for not driving. The backward thinking committee explained if City Cabs needed to get in touch with him, they would have had to contact the police who would have had to break into the radio circuit in order to give him a message. Because of this, they were threatening to withhold payment. At no time had I.B.M. complained how the part was delivered. After some thought, it was decided that he should be paid. Thereafter, it became the norm that if you got a London job, you should go to the garage on East London Street where the attendant would give you cash, then you drove to the airport, put the cab in the car park, left the meter running and then purchased a return on the shuttle. On your return, you stopped the meter and you were paid what was on it plus parking charges. The bonus was you got a meal both ways. But taxi drivers being taxi drivers complained that they were only getting paid waiting time, but it was unknown for anyone to hand the job back.

As a taxi driver you often pick up famous (and infamous) people. Generally speaking, they are often quite ordinary. This has led to the often overused expression "Do you know who I had in the cab today?" While some use their fame as a means of the driver not charging them, others wish to remain anonymous. Some treat you like a friend and will chat away on different subjects during the journey. One such was Billy Connelly.

Getting a radio job from the Traverse Theatre, which at the time was in the West Bow, I was told the fare was going to Stirling. On going into the bar to announce my arrival, I was told it was for Billy Connelly and he was in the bar and would be out in a few minutes. Returning to the cab, I settled down to wait. After a period of time the "Big Yin" appeared, opened the door and sat on the tip up seat behind me. He was full of apologies for keeping me waiting, explaining he was in the middle of a story. Off we set for his house in Drymen, with him sitting astraddle the tip up seat and telling me stories about life in the shipyards. I laughed so much I don't think we ever exceeded 30mph. When he paused for breath, I asked him why he had never replied to my letter and related the background to the story. Whilst working in Liberia, I was Chieftain of the Caledonian Society and another Scot had returned from vacation in Glasgow with some L.P's featuring a new comedian named Billy Connelly. As we had never heard of Billy Connelly, the Scot invited us to bring some beers, go to his house and listen to the L.P.'s. As we were making arrangements for our St. Andrew's night dinner, it was decided to write to Billy and invite him to be our guest of honour, all expenses paid for a week. But we never got a reply. Relating this story to Billy, he amazed me when he exclaimed "I remember that letter." When I asked him why he did not reply, his answer was, "I didn't know where it was and couldn't find it on a map." However, he did say he would include it in his upcoming book, 'Gullibles Travels.' He's a truly funny man.

The Bag Lady, as she became known, was an eccentric lady who would take a taxi anywhere. She always had matching luggage, ie two Tesco carrier bags, (one containing bundles of cash) a parrot in a cage and an aroma surrounding her like the kid in the Ready Brek advert.

When she first appeared on the scene, a night shift driver told her that the only taxis allowed to go out of town were the ones ranked in the Waverley Station which, at the time was operated by City Cabs. So, when she wanted a cab, she would get one to Waverley and then cross to the rank and then get in another. She was known to take cabs to the Highlands or the Lake District.

Getting her as a fare one day, she asked to go to Perth. On arrival in the station car park, she asked me to wait, got out and disappeared. She returned 5 minutes later with a parrot in a cage. She then told me to take her to Langholm, where our destination was a small caravan in a field miles from anywhere. There was never any quibbling about the price. She simply gave the driver what he asked for, but the second time you got her, you added a fiver on to buy air freshener to fumigate the cab when she got out.

One night I finished a shift and went to City Cabs garage to fuel up and have a coffee. The Howf was full of drivers doing what they do best, moaning about the public. When Blabs (V22) walked in and was asked what like a night he had. "Bloody grim! I picked up this smelly old bitch in the Waverley who asked to go to the St. James car park. Getting out she asked me to wait for a few minutes, "Aye right so I will." As soon as she was out of sight I swallowed what was on the meter and buggered off. The car was honking, I had to open all the windows to get rid of the smell."

At this point the other drivers 'in the know' did not enlighten him as to who she was. A few minutes later, George Kerr came in and announced, "What a strange game this is." He went on to explain that around 7.30pm, he dropped off a fare at the King James Hotel and while sorting out his cash, the door opened and a woman got in with a parrot in a cage and said, "Thanks for waiting. Will you take me to Lake Windermere?" She went into a carrier bag and produced a bundle of notes. She was a bit smelly, but I figured I can buy an air freshener. At this point everyone in the howf looked at Blabs and went into gales of laughter.

During the winter of 1978-79 the weather was poor and the country experienced heavy snow. Rab Skirving, being small in stature, also had small feet and was fed up getting his feet wet. He asked his wife to buy him a pair of Wellington boots, which she did. Next morning when going to start work, he walked across the car park to the taxi. As he walked, he was shocked to see his footprints had left an impression in the snow of Paddington Bear. Apparently, the only wellies available in the shops were in children's sizes, so she had to take them.

Rab would go on to be included in the Guinness Book of Records for the most consecutive appearances as Santa Claus at Murrayburn Primary School. This was a tradition he started when his daughter was a first-year pupil at the school.

He continued every year, even after his daughter became a teacher at the school. His final appearance was in 2015.

Rab died in 2016 and was a great loss to the cab trade for his sense of humour.

Edinburgh has many beautiful buildings. Three of the most impressive are schools.

I was taking an American gentleman to the airport one day and as we passed Fettes College, he asked me what the building was that looked like Snow White's castle. With tongue in cheek, I told him it was the local school and allegedly, attended by James Bond. I told him the same story about it being a local school when we passed Stewart Melville College. As we passed Donaldson's School for the Deaf, he was amazed and impressed by the grandeur of the building and grounds and asked what the building was used for. Trying to keep a straight face, I told him it was just the school the local children used. The American man then told me that 10% of management in the top 100 companies in America were Scots or of Scottish descent. He then added, "Now that I have seen the local schools, I am not surprised."

Many taxi drivers will go the extra mile to help older people but Big Stuart took it a bit too far. Stuart picked up an elderly lady and took her to Waverley Station. She told him she was going to stay with her daughter as she was getting a bit frail. Arriving at the station, Stuart drove up to the gate on platform 10 and helped the lady from the cab. He asked if she had her ticket and which coach she was travelling in. With the information she gave, he took her suitcase and helped her onto the platform, leaving the cab door open and the engine running. Finding the right carriage, he helped her into her seat which was situated in the middle of the coach and put her case on the luggage rack. The train was extremely busy with passengers trying to find their seats and taking off backpacks to stow in the luggage rack. Stuart could not get past them to alight from the train when there was an announcement that the doors were being shut and anybody not travelling should get off. Stuart did not hear it, and a few minutes later the train departed with Stuart onboard, first stop Newcastle. He managed to contact the train manager and explained the situation. Borrowing his phone, he called City Cabs to arrange for someone to take his taxi to the garage where he would pick it up on his return.

He arrived back five hours later, just in time for his change over. The good news was that East Coast trains did not charge him for his journey.

When lap dancing bar's were first opened, one of the most popular was the Liquorice Club on Home Street. The dancers mostly came from Newcastle and arrived on a Monday afternoon.

They would be picked up in the Waverley Station and taken to their hotel before going to the club. It became a daily job taking the girls from the hotel to the club and back again at night when the club closed. The girls generally stayed for a week before being replaced with fresh faces, not that any of the customers were looking at their faces.

When the European Union admitted more members, women from Eastern Europe arrived, changing the whole scene. It was not uncommon for some taxi drivers to be in the vicinity of the club when it closed to make sure they got one of the jobs. One night Richard won the prize and announcing his arrival to the doorman, awaited with great anticipation for the arrival of his fare. A stunningly beautiful blonde girl, wearing a low cut top and micro mini skirt got into the cab. Richard repositioned the rear-view mirror in order to get a better look at this vision of loveliness, and attempting to engage her in conversation. Richard enquired "Are you a pole dancer?" "No" she replied, "I come from Lithuania."

Before the advent of smokeless zones, when coal was the form of heating and sometimes cooking in most homes, coal merchants were a common sight on the streets. They had their regular customers requiring one or two bags a week.

The coal was delivered to the house in thick jute 1 cwt. bags carried on the back of the coal man. The coal man would grasp a top corner of the bag in each hand and hoist it onto his back. This was a very physical job, especially in streets consisting of tenements four or five stories high.

Mark Evans (V103) had been a coal man before coming onto the taxis.He started off with a horse drawn cart before progressing to a petrol driven lorry. Sitting on the rank one day he was relating stories of when he had a coal run in the Granton area. He mentioned that one of his men was a young Billy Codona (V86 and known to everybody as cowboy) and added the comment "He was the laziest bugger I ever employed." A few days later, I met cowboy in the garage and asked him if what Mark had said was true. Now cowboy was well known for his stories and he looked around and said "Yes, it was true." He then added "But I will tell you about him." He went on to say that one day while delivering coal on Lower Granton Road, they pulled into Victoria Square and Mark announced their arrival. This was done by shouting "COAL" at the top of his voice. His customers would then let him know how many bags they required. One of his regular customers was a well endowed lady who lived on the top floor of a tenement. On this particular day she was having a bath when she heard Mark shouting "COAL." She hurriedly wrapped a towel around herself and went to the window. As she opened it, she leaned out and shouted that she required one bag. At this point the towel slipped leaving her bare to the waist. Cowboy told us that Mark was on the second floor before he realized he had the horse by the ears.

At City Cabs garage was, what became part of the cab trade folklore, euphemistically called a rest room, but it was better known as the "howf." It was the site of the busiest vending machine in Scotland, which required it to be restocked twice a day and a mechanic on call 24/7 in case of breakdowns. This was where drivers met for a coffee and gossip was exchanged. To relieve the boredom on the night shift, quizzes were started with the first prize being a cup of coffee. During a discussion about various cartoon characters one evening, Tam Doyle stated that "Oor Wullie's" surname was MacDonald. This was met with howls of derision, but he insisted that in the second episode of the cartoon, P.C. Murdoch went to Oor Wullie's house and enquired of his mother "Is Wullie in Mrs. Macdonald?" The night shift was now split into two groups, those that believed Tam and those who didn't. The question now was how to find out the truth. This was solved by Wee Gillie, who producing the phone book announced, "We will ask D.C. Thompson." Looking through the phone book he found a number in Dundee and dialled it. The young lady who answered could not believe her ears when Gillie said "Tam Doyle has told us that Oor Wullie's surname name is MacDonald, is this true?" The young lady told him to hang on while she checked. Imagine the scene in the office where she would be telling her colleagues, "I've got a right nutter here." After five minutes she returned and said "I have checked all our records and Oor Wullie has never had a surname. Is there anything else I can help you with?" "Yes" replied Gillie "What are the names of the Twins and the Bairn in the Broons?" At this point the phone was slammed down so we never did find out.

John Graves was a cabbie who pulled more strokes than the Oxford rowing crew. He was also a stalwart of the kids outing, winning best dressed cab on many occasions. Indeed, in the 70's and 80's, the only time anyone else had a chance of winning was when John was away following his other passion, the Scottish football team, as a member of the Tartan Army.

John was a great football player, winning many trophies with ECATRA.

John and I were invited to meet with Richard McBrearty, the curator of the Scottish Football Museum which is part of the national stadium at Hampden Park. We were there to discuss the possibility of having a display of trophies and medals won by ECATRA. This was to be accompanied with the story of how it all began. The curator was fascinated by the story and was keen to have a permanent display, saying, "The story should be told." As part of the meeting he took us to the warm up area underneath the stand where there was a goal set up with some equipment. He explained that the equipment was used to measure the speed of a penalty kick. He went on to say that it had just been used by the Scottish Ladies football team and invited us to have a go. John did not need asking twice. Taking off his jacket and tartan scarf, he proceeded to take a kick. Richard then took a print out from the machine and told John his result. It was 2 mph slower than the slowest kick taken by the ladies' team. A completely devastated John left the stadium muttering "Bloody machine was not working properly! They can forget getting the trophies. Cheating bas**rds!"

John was very proud when his grandson Daniel became a football referee.

He would try to watch as many games as he could where Daniel was an official. After a match with Queens Park at Hampden, they went to the restaurant for the post match meal. In the car on the journey home, John asked Daniel the question "Who was the last man to lift silverware at Hampden?" After thinking for a minute Daniel replied, "The Hibs captain, Scottish cup, 2016." "Wrong" said John. Going into his pocket, John produced a teaspoon he had nicked from the restaurant.

R.I.P. John. A true legend.

The building at the junction of St. Stephens Street and St. Vincent Street was built as a church and due to the shape of the ground, entry was via a gallery, made possible by a flight of stairs from pavement level to the front door.

Taxi driver Brian, who was a bit over the top regarding his cab, insisted it must be washed every day and polished twice a week. It was rumoured that he traded in his cab when the ash tray needed emptying. He had to get the first of any new type of vehicle to be introduced.

One winter's night, while taking a fare down St. Vincent Street to Clarence Street, he applied the brake. Due to a hard frost, the cobblestones were like a sheet of glass causing the wheels to lock. This sent the cab into a skid, resulting in it mounting the pavement and climbing the steps causing severe damage to the front end. Brian radioed in to the fleet for help but before anyone could get there, a police car saw the taxi halfway up the steps and went to enquire what had happened. The same thing happened to the police car, skidding into the rear of the cab. When other cabbies arrived, Brian was a complete wreck saying over and over "Look at my cab! It's only a month old and that stupid cop just rammed me." Assessing the damage, it was the cumulative opinion that the vehicle was an insurance write off. This did nothing to calm Brian down. Alec Cadden then arrived on the scene. As he mounted the church steps he looked under the vehicle, then turned to Brian and asked him "What happened? Were you taking the cab in for a service?" At this point Brian lost it completely and burst into tears. Sympathy and regard for cabbies' feelings are in short supply among night shift drivers. The oft quoted statement seemed to be "Anyone looking for sympathy can find it in the dictionary between symmetry and symphonic."

Wee Tommy who fancied himself as a ladies man was having an affair with one of the telephonists in the office. He decided to take her to Spain for a week's holiday.

As a cover story, he told his wife that he was going on a golfing holiday with a group of cabbies.

While he was having a romantic time in Spain, his wife met a woman whose husband was supposed to be on the golf trip. During the conversation, Tommy's wife discovered that the other husband was not in Spain, but at work.

When Tommy and his paramour returned and were coming arm in arm through the "Arrivals Gate", they were confronted by Tommy's wife. Caught bang to rights, Tommy asked his wife how she had found out.

She replied, "You forgot to take your golf clubs."

Frank Walls recalled when he was working in City Cabs control room, the office manager, who was known to the trade as the Gonk, was teaching a new telephonist the correct way to answer a call. To demonstrate the procedure, he took the next call. "Hello City Cabs, can I have a taxi please?" Telephonist answered "Yes certainly, what's your name?" "It's sister Theresa." The telephonist then said "Thank you. Where are you?" Sister Theresa replied "I'm at 'The Little Sisters of the Poor' on Gilmore Place." (a charitable order of nuns). The telephonist then asked "Are you in the Bar or the Lounge?"

I got a radio job one evening, "Pick up Alec "Happy" Howden at St. Mary's Star of the Sea Club in Coatfield Lane. After he got in the cab, I asked him how the gig went. "No' very well" he replied. "It started off badly." He went on to explain that there had been a break-in at the club and thieves had stolen their television. To raise funds to purchase a new one, they were running a Fund Raising Night at which Alec was the star turn. As he walked out onto the stage, he noticed a shelf on the wall where the television had been situated. In the absence of the television on the shelf, it now held a statue of the crucifixion. Nodding towards the statue, Alec said "I see you got the bas**rd who stole the telly." He then said to me "I don't think I will be asked back." He continued to crack jokes all the way to his destination. A truly funny man.

Eddie Smeaton got a radio job one day from a stair on Bank Street (above what was then Christies the jewellers and now a Gold Brothers tartan tat shop). It was a regular job taking the lady to Jenners for lunch. She lived on the top floor, which was an attic conversion and with no call back in these days, the driver had to announce the arrival of the cab. Eddie who smoked about 40 fags a day, was completely out of breath after climbing up the five floors. When the lady answered the door he gasped "Is God in?" She reported him to City Cabs for cheek and he was given a week off the air. The good news was that she then started to use Central Radio Taxis.

Long time cabbie Stevie O'Reilly had suffered a heart attack and after a spell in hospital was recovering at home. Checking up on him one day by phone, he told me that he was getting better, but that day was not feeling so good. With his wife at work and his daughter at school, he was in bed resting. His voice started to get fainter and then stopped completely. All I could hear was the sound of laboured breathing. Shouting down the phone brought no response and I was in a dilemma as to the best course of action. I decided to phone the police in Dalkeith for assistance. Explaining the situation to the telephonist, I gave them Stevie's address. I was told that a patrol car was a short distance away and would check it out. Some ten minutes later the police phoned back to say he was ok and would be in touch shortly. A short while later Stevie phoned and explained what happened after the phone line went dead. His next door neighbour was working from home on his computer when his internet connection failed. Going next door, the neighbour asked Stevie if his connection was working. While standing at his front door, they were surprised when a police car with blue lights flashing came into the street and pulled up at Stevie's door. Jumping out, the policeman enquired if he was ok. Stevie, quite bemused, said he was ok, then asked the policeman want he wanted. After listening to their stories and trying to figure out what had happened, they all looked down the street and saw a British Telecomms line man up a phone pole. When asked what he was doing, the BT line man admitted he had disconnected the wrong wire.

As a cabbie you never know who you are going to pick up.

The term legend nowadays is often used to refer to people of mediocre talent and achievements.

But one man who truly deserved the accolade was Jim Haynes. An American who lived in Paris and held open house dinners every Sunday evening. Anybody could go, just let Jim know in advance.

While living in Edinburgh he opened the first paperback bookshop in George Square (now demolished but marked by a rhinoceros head on the wall). He played a big part in the founding of the Traverse theatre and the Edinburgh Fringe.

I picked him up one day from his hotel to take him to a book publishers office on Frederick Street. On the journey, as we were stuck in traffic, he was chatting away. He told me he was going to see a publisher who wanted him to write a guide book on Edinburgh. Quite facetiously I said, "Why get an American, living in Paris, to write a book on Edinburgh." I then added "It's already been done." I showed him a draft copy that I had in the cab. Sitting back and reading it, he told me that this was exactly what they wanted and as he did not have the time to do it, asked if he could take my manuscript and show it to them. A few days later the publisher phoned me and told me that they were interested, and could I supply more copy. That is how 'My Fare City' came to be published.

Since then I have written two other books "A Good Night Out "and "Cabs, Companies, Characters, the story of the Edinburgh cab trade."

I regret I never got the chance to thank Jim for his help.

It was with great sadness that I learned of the death of Jim Haynes in January 2021.

The pub trade and the taxi trade have been intertwined for a very long time through being each other's customers and over the years many bar staff became well known to drivers. In the days before the breathalyser it was not uncommon when going for a pub job to take the staff home, the driver was invited in for a drink, sometimes getting very friendly with the barmaids. Some of these people have entered into the folk lore of the City. Betty Moss, who for many years ran the Old Chain Pier dressed in a kimono, with bamboo framed glasses and wielding a sword stick, was one of them. She would stop serving and do a dance on the bar. At closing time she would call a cab to take her home, she lived on Trinity Crescent, nearly opposite the pub, so all the driver had to do when he picked her up was a U turn and she was home, but as she had the day's takings it was a smart move and the driver was always well paid.

Willie Ross ran the Oxford Bar as his own personal fiefdom since he took it over in 1935. He was positively eccentric with very strong opinions, very strongly expressed. He opened and closed the bar when he felt like it, closed it on a Saturday night, and also during the festival as he did not like the type of custom he would get. He also felt free to insult, curse and eject anyone who he took a dislike to. A great number of New Town residents felt the lash of his tongue, much to the amusement of onlookers. A young lady asked for a vodka and orange was told, "I don't do cocktails." My friend asked for a half pint of lager and was told, "I don't serve poofs." However, if when no one upset him, he was a fund of great stories.

Ranking alongside them was Maggie Rae. Maggie was voted Britain's rudest publican, a title she was justly proud of and who appeared on ITV Good Morning Britain to collect her prize. I asked her about appearing on the show and she said, "Ann Diamond was f**king lovely but that other bast**d, Nick Owen, was a pain in the arse." Her autobiography "Knickers Tae You! : The life and Times of Maggie Rae : Britain's Rudest Publican" was a collection of stories about the various pubs she had worked in. Maggie was well known to the cab trade as she was a regular user. Her stints in pubs became the stuff of legend. She ran her pubs with a strict 'no nonsense' approach and she always had a chair leg near to hand to use as a cudgel on anybody who caused her displeasure. If any licensed premises were causing concern to the brewery, Maggie would be sent in to restore order, which she did in a very short space of time, with the use of her tongue backed up with her cudgel. She was only about 5 feet 4 inches tall, but never let her lack of size stop her from ejecting anybody she thought would be a nuisance. Over the years she restored order to such salubrious establishments as The Old Vic, (now the Doghouse) Corn Exchange on Baltic Street, and the Candlemaker Arms, (Bar Salsa) which in the Edinburgh Pub guide was described as "the veritable pits." It was graceless, featureless and comfort less. The only entertainment being the gravel voiced barmaid, (Maggie) who in the space of thirty minutes threw out two customers, bawled out two more and three were refused service. All the while, a customer was trying to steal pies from the machine on the bar, which maybe was not the best idea as Maggie was known to dry her knickers on it. It was also described as a great cure for ethnic nostalgia and was Scottish drinking at its most desperate. One day, while taking her home, we were going up Liberton Brae when an ambulance passed us going down. It had blue lights flashing and sirens screaming. Maggie quite nonchalantly said "Hope it's my bast**d of a husband taken a heart attack." Arriving at her door, a man was in the garden and she looked up, and said "No such luck, the fu**ing sod is still breathing." True characters all.

Chapter 21

CONCLUSION

This book was written to give an insight into how the Taxi Trade started and how it has evolved through the years. The trade has faced many challenges but none more severe as the 2020 pandemic.

Taxi Drivers are known for their humour which is not always politically correct. They are also known for their charity work and their willingness to help others when necessary. One example of this was when some drivers got involved in taking medical staff to and from hospitals without payment during the Covid-19 lock down, when public transport was severely limited. The trade also stepped up to deliver food parcels to the vulnerable and made sure the elderly got to medical appointments.

As a large part of taxi drivers work involves carrying tourists from the airport or transport hubs to hotels and serving the hospitality industry, the effects of the pandemic were catastrophic. The year 2020 saw the Taxi Trade almost driven out of existence by Covid 19 and people's fear of infection due to close contact. The situation has had a devastating effect on the Taxi Drivers and others within the trade with many having to take any job they can to feed their families.

As it is a second career, many drivers are older and simply decided to leave the trade completely. Their knowledge and experience will be greatly missed and impossible to replace. It is a sad fact that the licensing authority did very little to help the trade in these severe times. While taxi numbers are restricted, the number of Private Hire Company (PHC) is unlimited and even during the worst of the crisis, the Council were still issuing licenses to PHC when it was clear that there was no work available.

This sad situation inevitably led to some PHC drivers breaking their licensing conditions and in many cases the law. Frustratingly to the cab trade, little or no action was taken. This has led to some in the trade to believe that it is the Council's intention to destroy what was once a great service and second to none.

As an illustration of how much the cab trade has fallen behind in earning potential. In the 1970's it was always calculated that the price of buying a plate was one and a half times the price of a new vehicle. Today that would be around £95,000-£ 100,000. With the "drop of the flag" equal to the price of a fish supper it is easy to see how the trade has stagnated. With overheads rising and earning potential falling the trend of offering large discounts must be questioned.

Hopefully, the future will bring better times for all in the Taxi Trade and everyone else who has suffered due to Covid 19.

Bob McCulloch passed his topographical test in January 1979.
He started driving in City Cabs when he purchased a cab and plate with the radio call sign V36
He became involved with the Children's outing, including a four year stint as treasurer.
For many years he contributed articles to Taxi Talk magazine.
Author of two books *My Fare City* and *A Good Night Out*. He is also the compiler and publisher of Thompsons Street Directory, known as the 'Taxi Drivers Bible.'
He qualified as a City tour guide in 1984 receiving many five star reviews. He organized classes for potential tour guides under the auspices of the Worshipful Company Hackney Carriage Drivers of which he became a member in 2005, gaining the Freedom of the City of London in 2006, the first Scottish taxi driver to do so. He became a Burgess of the City of Edinburgh in 2019 and joined the Incorporation of Baxters.
After retiring as a cabbie, he continued as a tutor at the Kerlin Taxi School,
a position he has held for over twenty years, and where he passes on his knowledge to potential taxi drivers.

Crest Worshipful Company Hackney Carriage Drivers
motto
With Knowledge We Serve

Throughout the whole Taxi Trade
Interest is focused on . . .

THE 2·2 LITRE
AUSTIN
DIESEL F.X.3.D. TAXICAB

**PRICE—
£1,041 10s.**

(F.X.3 Petrol Engine Taxicab-£936 10s.)

Sole London Concessionaires

MANN & OVERTON LTD
298 Wandsworth Bridge Road, S.W.6

Telephone   RENown 4484 (4 lines)

Printed in Great Britain
by Amazon